P9-CAN-834

Rockin' Steady

Walt Frazier
"Clyde"

Rockin'

Prentice-Hall, Inc. Englewood Cliffs, N.J.

Steady

A guide to basketball & cool by

Walt Frazier

and Ira Berkow

With an introduction by Bill Russell

Photography by Walter Iooss Jr.

Drawings by John Lane

Dedication

To my mother, brother and son

Acknowledgements

The authors wish to thank the following for their valuable assistance:

Paul Corvino, who supplied the glue to the original project.

Ralph Novak, Charles Miron, Arthur Sherman, Ross Gelbspan, Dave Hendin, Murray Olderman, Bob Cochnar, and Ernestine Guglielmo, who supplied much good taste to the manuscript.

Maria Juarez, Fran Gertler and Janice Graves, who supplied the magic to interpret the tapes.

Bob Metz, who supplied some much-needed time.

And Nancy, Ricky and Timmy, who supplied love.

Prentice-Hall International, Inc., London
Prentice-Hall of Australia, Pty. Ltd., North Sydney
Prentice-Hall of Canada, Ltd., Toronto
Prentice-Hall of India Private Ltd., New Delhi
Prentice-Hall of Japan, Inc., Tokyo

Library of Congress Catalog Card Number: 73/20933

ISBN: 0-13-782235-9

Printed in the United States of America

10 9 8 7 6 5 4 3 2 1

Planned & Produced by Sayre Ross Co., New York

Contents

11  Cool

27 

Defense

68  Offense

106

	min
Barnett	4
Bibby	14
Bradley	33
Frazier	57
Gianelli	16
Jackson	20
DeBuschr	51
Lucas	15

Statistics

108  Rockin' Steady : Game Day

133  A general guide to looking good, and other matters

Introduction by Bill Russell

When I was first asked to write an introduction to this book, my first thought was how to take up two or three pages of space talking about a guy I can sum up in a few words. The answer came to me in a flash: why not sum Clyde up in a few words.

Clyde is a super guy. To say he is a super ballplayer is redundant. His six years with the Knicks have earned him a place among the game's "greats," and his sneaky way with a ball has earned him the only half-kidding title, "Masterthief". The fans like Clyde not only because he plays good ball but also because he's reachable as a person . . . they like his funny wide-brimmed hats and easy laugh.

Read "Rockin' Steady" then. When did you last read a book by a sports figure that was so personal, that talks so freely about a man's emotions . . . fear, doubt, love for others. Clyde starts his book with a chapter he calls "Cool,"

Bill Russell (in playing days) tries to get a point across.

which tells you a lot about a man's philosophy, his attitude towards himself and others and life. It also makes clear, very clear, his love of the game which brought him recognition. He enjoys being a hero because he likes to think he's good . . . and he likes to play ball. Next to handling a ball and shooting for a basket, this book brings you closer than any I know to understanding what makes the game and, more importantly, what makes a player.

The player in this case is an extraordinary guy . . . a young man who gives of himself completely because that is what he wants most out of life . . . to give of himself completely. A young man who is very complex and yet relatively simple. Clyde-superstar. This book shows how an enormously talented and very rich young man from a poverty background moves in and out of night life in New York, how he gets ready for a game, how he goes into his act on the courts. On every page, too, you see how he manages to hold on to that marvelous ability to laugh at himself . . . to be serious about his sport but not about himself.

Walt's book tells how a young man can come to grips with being a superstar, sure of himself, and yet sometimes not so sure. And there are those that find it extraordinarily difficult to handle —the adulation, the pressure, the temptation, the lack of privacy . . . all the things that can make your life almost unbearable. Clyde handles it with aplomb, cool, detached indulgence. This is a book more, not really about a life, but a life style. Easy going, yet intense. Relaxed, cautious. But always knowing who he is and where he's at. And it's about the big games, the little games, the games within games, how he plays them, and how he thinks they should be played. Clyde is a winner. Even better, Clyde is a champion.

William J. Long

"We'd get a rebound and pass the ball out to Frazier—and he's not even on our team." Atlanta coach Cotton Fitzsimmons explaining a Hawk loss to the Knicks.

"Clyde is the only player I've ever seen I would describe as an artist, who takes an artistic approach to the game." Bill Bradley, New York Knick forward.

"I celebrate myself." Walt Whitman.

Rockin' Steady

OFFICIAL

Cool

I remember when I was a kid of 10 or 11 and I'd wash my sneakers with soap and brush almost every night so they would be bright and white and dry by morning. I remember being very exact how I laced them up when I went to play basketball in the dirt schoolyard in Atlanta. That was when my sneakers were the hottest item in my wardrobe.

I can remember how prideful I felt to wear the sneakers, and how I dug looking down and watching me walk in them.

I can remember playing in that schoolyard and trying to dribble and the ball would be bouncing this way and that way and off the rocks and pebbles and I'd hound the ball down. Then maybe it would bounce crazy and hit me in the nose. I can still feel that. And I can still remember that you'd have to be a magician to dribble the ball on that dirt court when it rained.

The setting is a lot different today from when I was coming up. But I have some of the same feelings. I still have to look particular when I play.

I tape my ankles while I'm still in my underwear because I want my uniform crisp and fresh when I go on the court. After taping I put my uniform on carefully. I make sure there are no bulges or floppy socks. My Pumas are laced just so.

Then I check out my face in the mirror. It takes about ten minutes. My hairline has to be just right. I pat down my 'burns. I mash down my 'stache—so the little hairs won't stick up and tickle my nose. I rake down my beard. I catch my profile. "Yeah, Clyde," I say, "You've got it." It relieves some of the pressure.

Before one game Randy, one of the Knick ballboys, walked by and caught me in my act. We'll joke a lot, and Randy called out, "Hey, get Clyde some ice, his head is swelling up." That relieves pressure, too.

I'm ready for the game now, ready to do something exciting like steal a ball—and still prepared for that funny bounce the way I learned to be in the schoolyard—and then I have it and drive for the hoop while 20,000 people are screaming.

I make the basket. I hear the roars. They come down at me like waves.

A lot has happened to me between now and then. But if I could start my life all over, I'd still want to be Walt Frazier. Clyde.

I have a son, which I've always wanted, Walt III. He lives in Chicago with my wife, who I've been separated from for several years. Walt is six years old, and he's cool. I took him to Kutsher's summer resort in the Catskill Mountains where I'm the head of the basketball camp. Took him up for a week. He could make baskets throwing underhand when he came. Then he saw the big kids shooting overhand and he started making baskets that way, too.

I've got a great long-term contract with the Knicks ($1.5 million over five years). I've got solid business deals and endorsements and good savings. I'm the president of Walt Frazier Enterprises, an organization for negotiating players' contracts and handling their money. It's the business I plan to devote full-time to when my basketball career

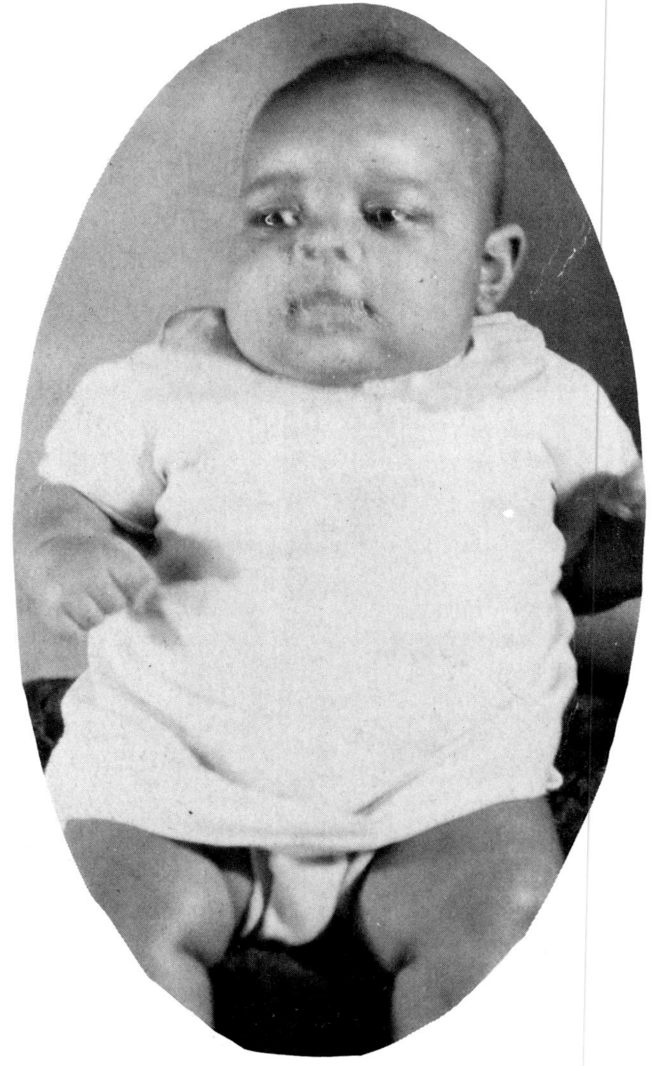

Clyde at two months.

ends. I've got a good business manager, Irwin Weiner. We got together three years ago when I had like $4,000 left in my bank account. I had a hair-styling business and it flopped. I was worried. I didn't know what to do with my paychecks. So I spent the bread. Things have changed.

My interests are growing. It's not like the previous years where basketball was everything—I needed it to eat. But playing basketball is still important because there are not many other things I like to do as much. I get joy just working out sometimes, just feeling the ball.

When I'm training in the summer, running on roads, I visualize playing in the Garden. I run two miles in the morning. It's not too exciting the first mile. But then I visualize being Clyde the superstar and wanting to be the best and I keep running. The game is close. I make a steal, score a basket, we're in the lead. I can hear the crowd in my mind. I run harder.

What more could I ask? I've got a great following. I have a few good friends. I've got enough money to buy anything I want. I wanted a Rolls-Royce. Bought it. I wanted a full-length, $5,000 black Ranch mink coat to go with it. Bought that. I bought my family in Atlanta a five-bedroom $58,000 home in a beautiful wooded area. It's about four miles from our old neighborhood. But it's so far away that when you drive there at night rabbits run across the road.

I'm not battered up. I don't have a lot of scars and bruises. I've never been hassled with injuries. Never had a major operation. So I'd say I've been very lucky.

The way my life is now, I'm all rock. I wake up in my penthouse apartment in the morning and usually I bang on what I call my go-go music, like James Brown or Shaft or The Temptations. I'm almost never bored. Someone said that being Clyde is enough for Frazier. Well, I'm happy most of the time. I want to move. Like the feel I have when driving a car at seventy, eighty miles an hour for a hundred miles. I'm rockin' steady.

In college I had a lot of jazz albums. That was my mood. I smoked a pipe. Now if I want to be frontin' it I'll smoke one of those long thin cigars.

In college I just meditated—thinking, hoping I'd be the way I am now. Hoping I'd be there one day. Hoping I could be a professional basketball star. There was a time in my life, if I would have been drafted eighth by a pro team I would have been happy. I didn't think I had the ability to be a professional. Well, maybe I thought it, but then every year when the basketball magazines came out you'd read about all those colleges and there are like 2,000 guys ahead of you, and your name isn't in that book. So you figure, how are you going to make it? And you're playing for a small school like Southern Illinois University. I didn't realize I was good enough until the National Invitational Tournament in New York in 1966. I was playing against what I thought was top competition. I was standing out, most valuable player. That was really when I thought I was good enough. You never know. A lot of players are paper players. They get a lot of publicity. They're not that great. I was very naive to a lot of things.

But I was lucky. I've always been lucky. I came to New York and eventually met some straight people. They pulled my coat as to what was going on. Made me aware of the good deals You meet a lot of shady characters. A lot of athletes, they get taken fast.

I came to the Knicks as first draft choice. But they had five guards. It really looked bad for me. Then guys started getting traded and I got a chance to play. But at first, man, I was such a chump on the court I cried. I was supposed to be a great defensive player and some guys made me look like a stupid fool. My offense was poor, too.

Then one night it was like a light was finally shining in the darkness. On defense, I nailed my man, and I started making baskets. I started seeing the open man—passing to the open man. I got confidence. It was like I had been dribbling before with my head down all the time.

Just being in the Big Apple, and everything that I hoped would happen has happened. Financially, clotheswise, being Clyde and all that stuff. In any other city I might not be Clyde. I don't know. New York is the mass media. It's where it all happens. I have two images, which is good. Fashion image and basketball image. I'm all-pro guard and *Esquire* magazine's fashion panel named me the "Best Dressed Jock." (I was also picked by *Pageant* magazine as one of the 10 Sexiest Athletes. Wilt Chamberlain was upset because he wasn't picked. He thinks he cuts a pretty dashing figure. He said there are a lot of girls who would vote him the sexiest athlete. And Frenchy Fuqua of the Pittsburgh Steelers wrote a letter to *Esquire* because he felt insulted they didn't name him one of the 10 Best Dressed Jocks. You can see that this 10 Best stuff can get pretty tense.)

Most guys are just basketball or football. Clyde is a title. It's different. It's a style. I can dig it.

The Clyde Style

I got the title "Clyde" from Danny Whelan, our trainer. It's funny. I bought this hat, the first Clyde lid. I bought it in Baltimore when I was a rookie. I went shopping in every town I went to. Spent almost $10,000 in clothes that first year. Nearly went busted. Well, I saw this wide-brim hat. I don't like small-brim hats on me. They don't look good. This lid cost $40. Most guys would never pay $40 for a hat. It was brown velour. When I used to wear this hat, all the guys in the NBA laughed at me. I can remember once we were in the Detroit airport. I had the hat on and guys were standing in the corner laughing. Guys on my team and guys on the other team, too. At the time nobody was wearing wide-brim hats like that. They made me feel so stupid that I almost stopped wearing those hats. But I just decided to wear what I want to wear.

After the Bonnie and Clyde movie came out there was a big boom in wide-brim hats and everybody was wearing them. They started calling me "Clyde" when the movie broke.

Once threadin' up like Clyde almost got me in trouble. I walked into my bank in Manhattan with my hat pulled down over my eyes. I wore a brown pin-striped suit with wide lapels. It was like the gangster look. The guard didn't recognize me. And I went to that bank all the time. I could feel eyes watching me. It was a funny feeling. Nobody said anything to me.

I had a bag, an attache case with just some papers and stuff in it. The players kid me that I'm carrying a sawed-off shotgun in it. The guard finally recognized me. "Oh, hello, Mr. Frazier . . . nice day." I guess it was the bag that threw him off.

You know, the way you play on the court, that's the way people expect you to be off the court. My hands are so fast, I'm so quick, that Bill Hosket, a former teammate, said, "Clyde is the only man who can strip a car while it's going forty miles an hour."

In a cocktail lounge once a glass slipped and I nabbed it in midair without spilling a drop. I do that a lot with most things that are falling. It's spooky how quick I am. It's just instinct. It's nothing you can practice. A natural cool.

Cool is my style. I almost never show any emotion on the court. A guy might harass me and it might be working, but if you look at my face, I always look cool. So they never know what I'm thinking.

Some cool is natural, but a lot of cool is learned. I learned that trick of not showing emotion from Elgin Baylor when I was a rookie. In one game I put on this fierce look when I was guarding him. I got up on him. I applied pressure. I went into this tough stance, gritting my teeth, waving my arms—to be scary. Elgin, he looked at me like, "Hey, young-blood, what you think you doin'?" Then he went into his moves like I wasn't there. He nearly blew my mind. I thought I was a strong player and he destroyed my ego. But I learned I could psych out an opponent by not letting him see he's making me jittery.

I think I began getting cool when I had to learn how to change my baby sisters' diapers and how to burp the babies. I'm the oldest of nine children

Santa Claus, with my sister, Mary, and me. She was 8, I was 10.

in the family. I have seven sisters and one brother. When guys in the neighborhood find out you're changing diapers, the trick is to make them think that, yeah, he-men do that all the time.

I was always a homebody when I was a kid. I was shy. In high school I'd go to dances and I'd be a wallflower. One reason is that when I tried to dance in my house my sisters would giggle and say, "What's *he* doin'?" I didn't come out of that until I was a sophomore in college. I was at a party and a slow record came on—I waited for the slow records. So now I asked a girl to dance. Then the record changed to a fast beat. I was stuck on the floor! I had to make up some moves quick. I was shocked. That was the start of my dancing career.

The first athlete who I thought was really cool was a baseball catcher for Chattanooga in the Southern Association. Chattanooga played my home town Atlanta Crackers. All the guys saw this catcher play with his right hand in his back pocket. We didn't realize he was just trying to protect his bare hand from foul tips. So the next day every kid in the neighborhood wanted to be a catcher, with one hand behind his back.

In high school sports I was the leader. The guard in basketball, the quarterback in football, the catcher in baseball. Like on the Knicks, I'm the playmaker. I'm the guy with the ball, and they're depending on me not to lose my cool.

And the title, Clyde, fits my daring style of play, stealing balls and gambling all the time and dribbling behind my back to escape pursuers.

But a funny thing, I'm quick but I'm slow, too. I mean, I run 100 yards in eleven flat—with the wind at my back. In high school football it was embarrassing doing the wind sprints because the coaches made me run with the linemen, and everybody laughed. My hands are small and kind of weak. I can't even palm the ball. I'm not even a great jumper. In college I played forward at first and everybody was jumping over my back and snatching rebounds away. I got stronger lifting weights and I learned positioning, which made me a better rebounder.

(From the David T. Howard High School year book, 1963: Hazel Jackson and Walter Frazier, voted most popular and voted most athletic in senior class.)

So I had to make up for my physical drawbacks by playing it cool. I play so cool now, in fact, that I hardly sweat on the court. Willis Reed will drop maybe twelve pounds in a game. I'll maybe lose a pound. That's all.

It's like when I'm warming up. I just shoot to get the feel, then I dribble along the side until I know I'm ready. I don't sweat until the game starts—and I often don't sweat even then. I'm sure sweating has a lot to do with natural body functions, too. Some guys sweat more than others naturally. But cool helps. So does pit juice.

Pit juice is what some of the players call underarm deodorant. Before a big game, or the first game of the season, games when I'm feeling the extra tension, I might be sweating a little more than usual. I don't like to sweat. So I squirt some juice in my pits to absorb the sweat.

Cool is a quality admired in the black neighborhoods. Cool is a matter of self-preservation, of survival. It must go back to the slave days, when oftentimes all a black man had to defend himself with was his poise. If you'd show fear or anger, you'd suffer the consequences. Today, the guy respected in the ghetto is the guy who resists the urge to go off—who can handle himself in a crisis, who can talk his way out of a fight.

Cool also provides a kind of community defense in the ghetto. It's used when we're faced with group adversity. Sometimes it's used against the cops, who have often been suspect by blacks. I remember when I was growing up in Atlanta, and I'd come home and see squad cars on my block. The cops would be asking after someone. But the people would be hush-hush. Nobody knows where the guy is, when everyone saw him run and crouch behind the stairwell. And all I'd be doing was watching and listening.

Some people might think cool is a retreat from true feelings. But sometimes keeping a cool is the most sensitive thing to do. It's like the kid in a ghetto who sees his best friend's mother have to go into the streets to meet men in order to make enough bread to feed her large family, since the

A summer run.

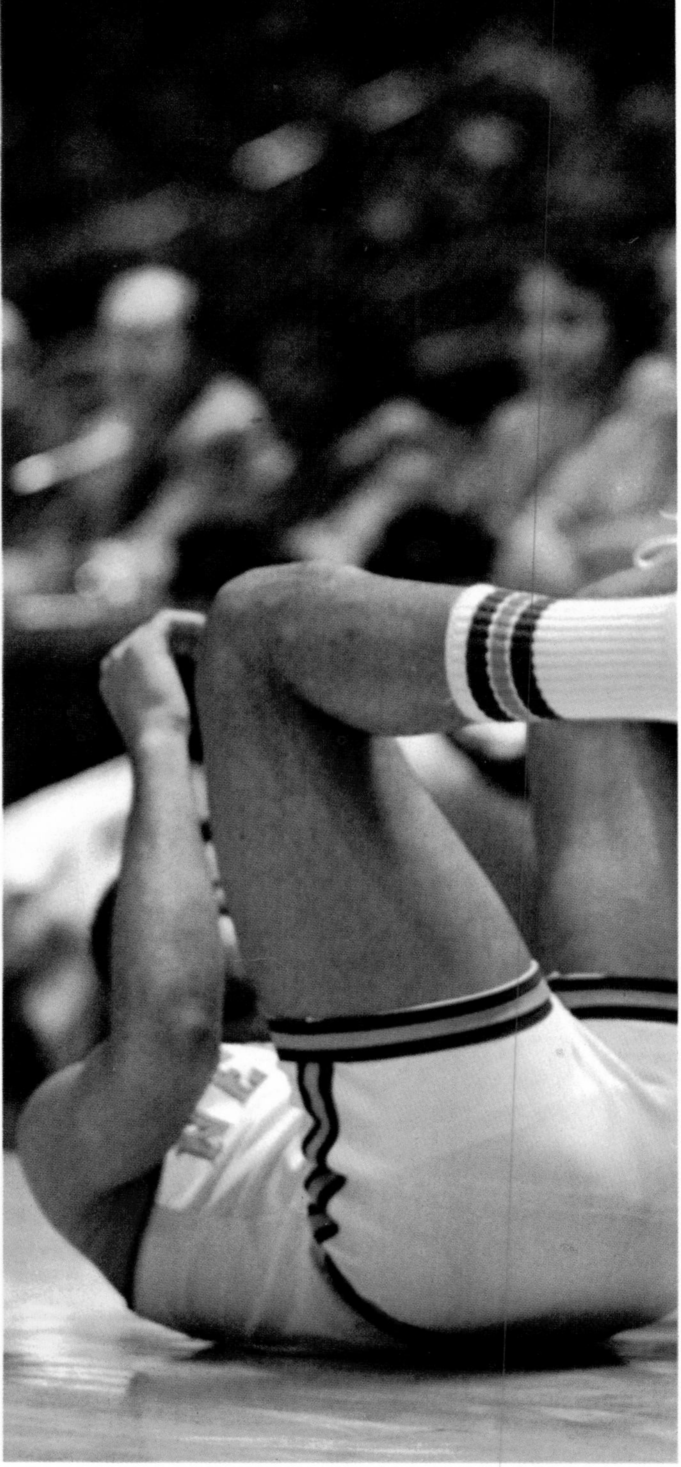

father has cut out. Well, the kid walks on the other side of the street so the mother doesn't see him, and then he never says anything to anybody about what he saw. If it got out, the other kids would tease his friend forever.

And I often like to stay neutral in discussions with people, especially teammates. Taking sides can cause hassles.

Cool I think is reactions, reflexes and attitude. You got to feel out the situation. You can't be out of control. I think I'm cool—most of the time.

I don't talk a lot, don't like to travel with an entourage. I've always been a loner. Always been my own man. When I go to a nightspot I don't try to play royalty. I don't walk in and say, "Run the bar, Clyde is here," and act loud. I just get lost within the people. And most people I meet say that they never thought I was a basketball player because I walk very slowly. I guess that is a carryover from playing the game cool, and trying to conserve energy.

Even though I'm quiet, it's very seldom I'm at a loss for words. That's part of cool, the reactions. I see and meet a lot of guys who try to be smart with me. Then I come back with a cooler answer. Like Howard Cosell. I was on his show once and he was saying," We have Walt Frazier here and he came up from Atlanta a poor kid" and Howard went on through a whole routine about my life and he ended it with something like, "Clyde, your career's been full of luck to attain your position." And I said, "Right, Howard, very similar to yours." All the TV guys there just broke up. He had no comeback.

Another time I scored 43 points, the first time in my pro career I went over 40. I hit everything. It was amazing. I almost didn't have to look and I just kept hitting all net. After the game I had all these reporters around me. One asked, "Clyde, aren't you supposed to be the one passing the ball?"

I said, "Yeah, our coach tells me I'm supposed to hit the open man. Well, tonight I was the open man."

USUALLY COOL

But like I say, I'm cool only most of the time. Once I had on these new $75 leather cowboy boots. First time I ever wore them. I came into the locker room before the game and tried to take them off. They wouldn't come. They were stuck. Willis had to help me yank them off. It was embarrassing. What really was bad was when I got home. I didn't have Willis then. I almost broke my arm pulling them off. Never wore them again.

Once I thought I had come up with a great new thing to outslick the defense. It was when a guy was going to give me an intentional foul, a common late-quarter strategy move at one time. You'd get one free throw instead of getting a chance to make a basket. Usually a defensive player just came over as you dribbled across the midcourt line and he sort of hugged you.

Well, I figured that if I'm going to get hugged it should be worth a two-shot foul. So this one time, while the defensive player was grabbing me as I crossed the line, I threw up a 40-footer. But the ref didn't call the two-shot foul. He didn't call anything. The crowd didn't utter a peep as the ball went flying over the backboard. I felt like the dumbest guy ever born.

Cool is having an attitude, too, of how you carry yourself. Especially in pain. That's the time you really should be cool, because if you stay in the game, you don't want the other team to know how hurt you are. They'd try to take advantage of it.

First I try to get under control. I know it's painful.

I remember a time I got hit in the eye. I was on Dick Snyder. He went in and dunked the ball and when he came down his elbow hit me in the head. So when I fell I was in great pain but when I was lying on the floor I crossed my legs, like I was in an office waiting for an appointment. I wasn't kicking the floor when I knew I was hurt. Some guys would be rolling over and moaning. When I get hurt I just lie down, relax. When I saw blood I didn't panic. The trainer ran over with a dry towel and I said, "Wait a minute, put some water on it." I was still under control. I knew what I was doing. I knew it was an accident. I didn't get mad at Snyder. I needed a few stitches. And so now I'm lying on the operating table. The doctor is over me and I'm just talking casual to him. "Doc, am I going to still be beautiful?" I've seen some guys get shots to quiet them down before they get stitched. But I make little jokes. The atmosphere is relaxed. People laugh. Then the doctor gets serious and I just get quiet and he sews me up.

My chicks, they're cool, too.

Once I made the mistake of giving tickets to two girls and they sat next to each other. I thought I was being cool. I played one of my worst games. I kept seeing both girls and worrying. It seemed wherever the ball went I could see them. I saw that they had the rocks in their jaws. But they never looked in each other's eyes. Never said a word to each other. When the ball went down this way, I saw one girl looking at the other. When the ball went back that way, the other girl was looking at her. I wasn't watching the game either. I was watching them. I'll never pull a trick like that again. Not only because I lost concentration and played bad, but I don't want to hurt the feelings of somebody.

Style is important in defense, too, in how you carry yourself. I've made guys feel so frustrated, like they were handcuffed, but they've never got mad at me. They know I never do anything dirty sly. I don't start talking to them either when I think I have them on the string. My philosophy there is, let sleeping dogs lie. It's like if you beat a team by a hundred points, you always say, "Well, they had a bad night." You don't really say they're no good, because teams remember that. And like in the playoffs particularly, players look for something to get them up. When West was off in the 1972 playoffs, I just said that he was off. I didn't say it was my defense or whatever I was doing.

At Southern Illinois. I didn't think I had the ability to be a professional.

In my rookie season, guarded by Satch Sanders of Boston.

It wasn't so long ago that I was like that kid, playing in a schoolyard.

I don't like to rely on trickery, on or off the court. I like to play a basic-type game. I use fakery, but not trickery. I like the game too much to rely on stepping on a guy's toes or holding his shorts when he jumps. After the game, I take a little longer dressing, especially when I played well. I sit down and read the statistics sheet of the game. See what happened. See how you did. It's a great feeling to know you really produced. Then you start thinking about some of your great moves, and you think about the next game. Sometimes I can hardly go to sleep at night, I'm so thrilled about tomorrow. Sometimes after a game I'll go to a nightclub and dance into the night—if we aren't playing the next day. I'm unwinding. Dancing is great for that.

Losing is sometimes different. I remember we lost to Baltimore in the 1971 playoffs. I couldn't sleep all night. I kept rerunning that last game in my head, up and back, like a movie projector. But I don't let anything get me down for long. I was cool the next day.

When the season is over, after two or three weeks, you want to touch the ball again, just run your fingers along the grain. It's like something you've had and you miss. So maybe you go out to a park and shoot for twenty minutes. Or sometimes if you're running across the street, it feels good just to run. I kind of miss it.

When I'm not playing, not in top shape, my food doesn't even taste good. That's why I'll always be in shape, always watch my weight and what I eat. I tell people, "How would a fat Clyde look!"

Being Clyde has some disadvantages. I don't have many private moments in public. People always want autographs. People think you should be thrilled to give them an autograph. It can be a bore. But then I think back to when I wasn't Clyde the superstar and I think it's better to have it than not to have it. So this is what everybody wants, the notoriety, and once they get it they start to abuse it, start walking on people. So I try to be courteous to everybody. I try to be conscious of another person's feelings. I try to put myself in their place. Some guys say "get away from me" to fans. I never do that. If I don't feel like signing autographs I'll say I don't feel like signing. I always give them a courteous out so they won't feel embarrassed.

Another thing about being Clyde, the cool loner, is I sometimes miss family life. When I come home to my empty apartment and I smell the cooking next door, I get to thinking about my family. I miss my son a lot. I wish I lived with him so I could take him to games in New York. That would be a trip, man. I take him to games when I get to Chicago. He's jumping all over. I think about taking him for drives through Central Park in my Rolls. Sometimes I'll see a television program where a father and son are doing things together. It makes me feel sad.

I think I relate best to young kids. Like at Kutsher's camp, I'll call the kids chump, they call me chump back. I tell them how great I am. They say to me, Jerry West is best. Or Pistol Pete. But we're just kidding. We get along good. Kids are real. You can't fool kids. Clyde Frazier fans, they're my fans to the end. Adults, they're shaky. Adults ride with the winner. If you lose you're a bum. But kids live and die with you. They make excuses for you.

When Julius Erving came up to Kutsher's for a day and beat me 4 games to 2 in one-on-one, the kids said, well, Clyde, he's taller than you. Or you'll beat him the next time. Or you just probably had an off day. Others said Clyde is still the best guard. Julius, he's a forward. Stuff like that. They'll always find a way out for you. That's a nice feeling.

I love kids. They don't know how to be phony. Like one day in the Catskills I picked up three kids hitchhiking. They got into my maroon El Dorado Cadillac (my "Clydemobile" before I sold it for the Rolls). The kids, they sank into the white leather seats. They were coming from playing ball somewhere. They were quiet. I got a feeling they knew who I was. But they didn't say anything. Cool cats. I didn't say anything either.

I stopped where they asked me to. They thanked me, very polite. They rolled out. I started to drive off and I looked into my rear-view mirror and I saw them jumping up and down, throwing their ball and towels in the air and they were slapping palms. That was cool, too.

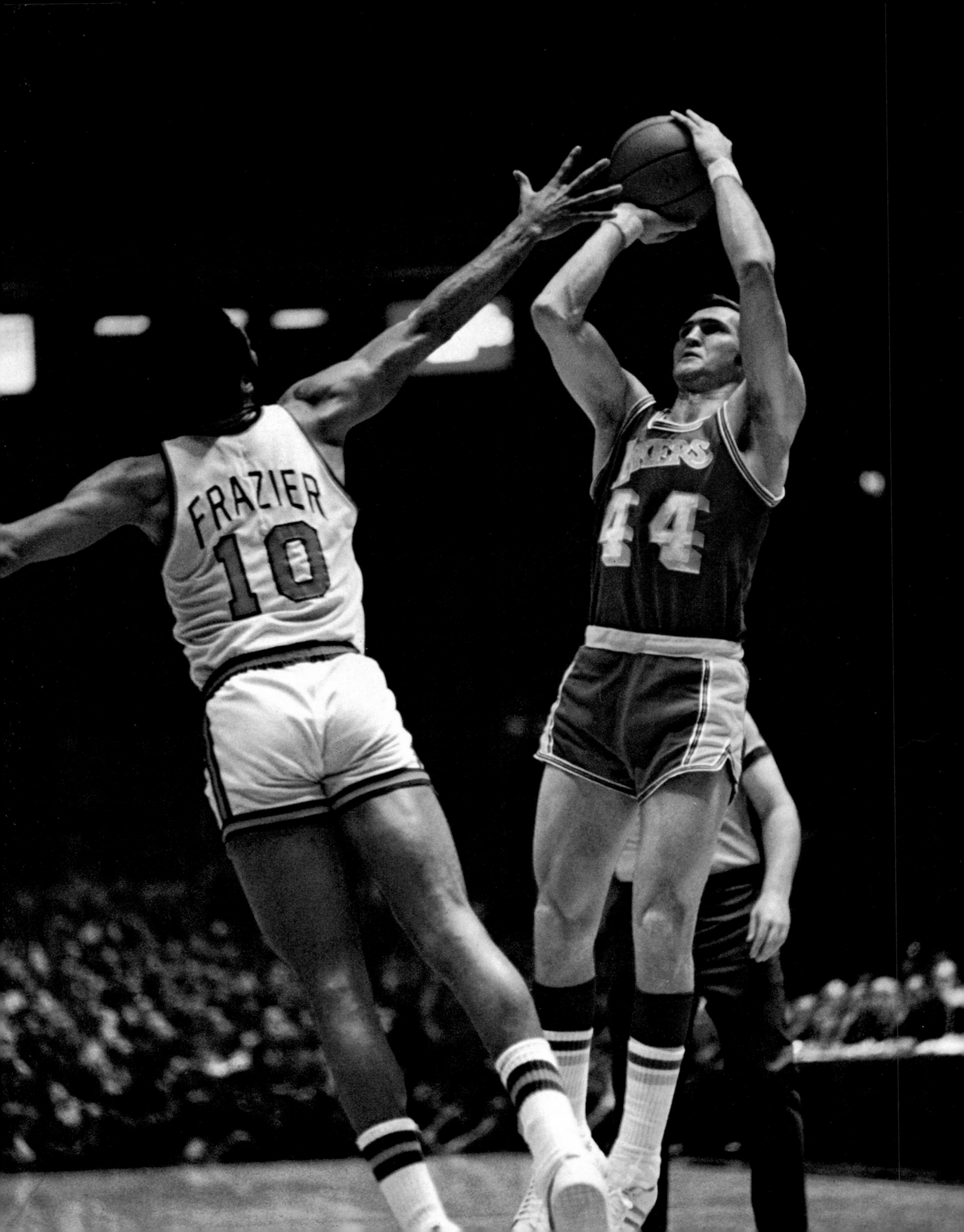
FRAZIER
10
44

Defense:

"Everyone Has a Certain Rhythm that He Dribbles to."

When I play defense, I expect the worst. I'm alert. I expect my man might go up to shoot anytime. Or a guy might set a pick on me. It's like when I'm driving a car. I always anticipate a guy cutting in front of me, so I drive in the middle lane. That gives me a better chance if I have a blowout. You now have two lanes to fizzle into. But if you're driving on the outside or inside you might run right into a rail.

I never expected the worst to be so bad as the first time I guarded Hal Greer. It was 1967, when I was a rookie. I came into the league with a deserved reputation as a great defensive player. But Hal Greer killed me. I never forgot that. He had a move where he faked and jumped into you. I knew he was beating me. I wasn't set. I wasn't relaxed. I was jittery. I fouled out after about five minutes. I remember crying, I was so embarrassed.

I knew I was better than that. I went through that kind of thing a lot during my first year. I had to try to analyze what I was doing wrong. I figured out that I kept letting Greer come to his right, like he likes to do. So I started forcing him to his left. I know he likes to shoot from the top of the key, so I forced him down into the corners. I had success with that.

Satisfaction is really seeing a team crack under pressure, begin to throw the ball away, dribble off their foot. You can see frustration in a guy's face. He is frowning and he looks aggravated, uneasy. It starts from your defense. And that's where my steals come in. Steals are the worst thing in the world for a team. It's demoralizing when the other team all of a sudden gets an easy basket. Two in succession. Now I can't stay away from the ball. I pick off another ball. The other team calls time-out. You come back to the bench and the crowd is standing and roaring. It makes me jingle inside. You got to be dead not to feel it. And that rally is usually all we need to pull away from the other team.

I've influenced the ballgame from the guard position. That's never been done before. Guards had never been able to change the tempo of the game. It had always been the big man, especially on defense. A guard like Bob Cousy might make some spectacular steals, but only one or two in a game. I was stealing ten, twelve every game. One game in 1971 against Atlanta I made something like eight steals in a row in the third quarter. I was about to collapse. I wanted to whisper to their guards how to dribble and pass the ball.

It really started happening for me in 1969-70, when we won the NBA championship. I made a lot of steals and teams were really trying to keep the ball away from my man. In key situations my man didn't have the ball, and usually I was guarding the top man. They made their guards spread out. It took the team out of its offensive pattern.

The most extreme case was what Detroit did. They stuck my man, Howard Komives, in a corner. The NBA had a stupid rule then that the defensive man had to be no more than six feet away from the man he was guarding. When I started to back off Komives and get back into the game, Komives would holler to the refs, "Who's Frazier guarding?"

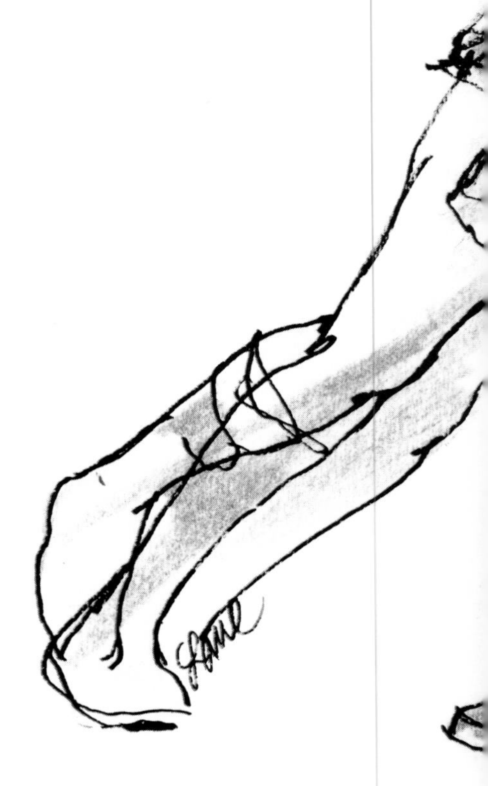

I make my move to steal the ball as soon as it leaves the dribbler's hand.

NEW YORK
18

WILLIAMS
7

That was when the publicity started about how fast my hands are, and how I can catch two flies at a time. A guy once told me about a friend who was so fast he could catch three flies at one time. Not bad, I told him, my trouble is that flies have heard about me. They don't come around anymore.

My defense began in college, when I didn't make grades one year, what would've been my junior year.

The coach, Jack Hartman, kept me in practices to just play defense. The whole year, nothing but defense. No offense. So I wanted to destroy the varsity's whole attack. Me and four other scrub guys. We cut the varsity out. They couldn't score. I got some pleasure getting back at the coach for not letting me play offense. Some guys would never have gone through what I did. Screw the coach and quit the team. But I said in my mind, since I gotta do it, I might as well, you know, do it.

When I made the NBA first-team all-defensive team in 1970, I got more votes than almost anybody—including Bill Russell. And Russell said, "You couldn't do any better than vote for Walt Frazier."

That was a thrill. Until Bill Russell came into the game, the game was basically a run-and-shoot game where most teams would just outscore the other team. Nobody relied on defense. When Russell came in as center in 1956, he intimidated people on defense. He led the Celtics to eleven NBA titles in thirteen years. Now the trend is defense. Not just in basketball, but in baseball and football.

I think the Knicks had a lot to do with making defense really popular—being in New York and getting a lot of ink for our team defense. The Russell defense was more like Russell and four other guys. Ours was a team defense, all five guys helping out.

At one time people said nobody appreciates a defensive player. So most guys, they just had eyes for the basket. But I found that whenever you get

Wilt sets pick for Jerry West. Jerry Sloan of Bulls fights through.

respect it's a great honor. It's enough reward for me that teams would keep the ball away from me, afraid I might steal it, or blaming their defeat on my steals.

To play tough defense you have to have hustle, desire and pride in not letting anybody score on you. I hate for anybody to score on me. But it's impossible to stop. I look at it this way: If I score 25 points and my man scores 25 points, what have I accomplished? So I try to keep my man well below what I score.

And the fans are getting to appreciate defense, at least in New York. Maybe a lot of fans don't go wild when you're not letting your man get off a shot. But I think more and more people are getting conscious of steals and blocked shots and picking off passes. Like in the Garden, the game gets tight, the first thing they scream is "Dee-fense, Dee-fense." They don't yell "Of-fense." That doesn't jingle nothin' inside.

Fundamentals

One thing about defense, you can never be off. You can be good on defense every night. On offense, you can make ten shots in a row one night, next night nothing. To be consistent on defense, you need to be alert and to have control of some fundamentals.

Basically, the same techniques apply to guards, forwards and centers.

1. I'm almost always facing my man and I'm always either between him and the basket or between him and the ball.

2. I see the ball. I know where it is. And I see my man. Even if he goes into a corner—then I slide off him to an angle as far as I can get back and still see him and the ball. I'm using peripheral vision and sort of looking in the middle between the ball and the man, but still seeing both.

Don Chaney sweeps in for a score, despite me.

3. Defense is reaction. You can't make a move on defense until there's a move on offense.

I anticipate on defense, after studying my man and his moves. That makes it easier for me to keep up with a lot of guys. But too many guys overanticipate. They're too fast, too much in a rush. They go for too many fakes.

4. Defense is mostly footwork. I don't like to use hands on my man. I think it's the lazy way, or the defensive player *thinks* he's taking the lazy way out. But I think it has the reverse effect because you're not as alert as sticking to footwork. I like to keep my man in suspense, wondering where I'm lurking, until he stops his dribble. Then you can wave your hands over him all kinds of ways.

5. I don't like switching on man-to-man, either. I think that's lazy, too. I like to guard my man because I've got pride in trying to keep him from scoring. (I don't like zones for the same reason.)

6. Position in defense is the most important thing. Stay balanced. Knees bent comfortably. Your back is a little lowered in a staggered stance. One foot about 4 or 5 inches in front of the other (doesn't matter which foot is forward, whichever is most comfortable). Legs are about shoulder-width, weight evenly distributed on the balls of your feet, head up.

7. Hands are comfortably out in front of you, palms up, like you're about to catch a beachball. Elbows about waist-high. A lot of high school coaches teach that you should have your arms way out. I feel like I'm off balance that way. So I figure if my hands are out easy and if he shoots I can still get my hands up fast. But maybe that's because of my quick hands. If a guy finds that his hands are down and his man is getting shots off, then I'd suggest he get his hands higher to begin with.

Hal Greer fakes. I jump. He once brought me to tears with that move.

PHILA
15

8. I give guys little flicks to see if it irritates them when they're dribbling. Maybe they get upset when I'm jerking at them.

9. Slide. Never cross your feet when guarding a man in the shooting range. You're beaten right away if you cross your legs because you've lost a step and all he needs is a step. Some defensive guys panic. They got to bump the man and try to slow him down, whereas I try to beat my man to where he's going by sliding. Of course, when you're trailing a guy who has slipped past you downcourt, then you run like Bob Hayes.

10. Try not to let a dribbler penetrate (get in around the foul lane). Even if he doesn't score, he disrupts the team defense because he got around you and somebody else has to pick him up. It's like a bad automobile driver. He might not get into an accident but he causes a lot of 'em.

Slide on defense

11. Never let a man drive baseline. If a guy goes baseline you should force him to stop and make him turn back. When a man drives you, get your body in front of him. And at the baseline you can step on the line if you want, to prevent him from coming on. The worst he can do is take his drive into the middle, where you can get help.

Don't cross your legs on defense

12. Everybody has a weakness. Study your man to find his.

13. What hand is he? That's the first thing I know about the guy I'm guarding. When I coach the kids at Kutsher's summer basketball camp I see them guard someone all game and at the end I'll ask, "What hand was he?" They didn't know if he was right-handed or left-handed. My philosophy on that is, if the guy is right-handed that's his best hand, so I try to force him to his left. Doing this I have a better chance of keeping up with him. I don't say it's 100 percent, but your man won't be as effective. When I guard a guy I always give him one alternative—that is, to go either to his right or his left. But if you are directly in front of him he can go either way. So I usually take one away from him.

14. I don't look at a man's eyes when I'm guarding him. His eyeballs could be going one place but the rest of him might go somewhere else. I usually watch his chest or I watch his beltbuckle. I should say I watch anything but the guy's eyes and the ball. It's those two that he can fake you with. But like in every rule, there are exceptions. And I've got at least two.

a. I sometimes watch a passer's eyes to see if he telegraphs his pass. (Although a sharp passer might look one way and pass another.)

b. If you happen to lose the ball and you're running to pick up a defensive man, you might be able to see the ball coming in the guy's eyes. Jerry West did that against the Knicks in a game in the 1972 playoffs. He was running to pick up a man and had both hands up over his head. The pass landed in his hands. He actually caught the ball without ever seeing the ball coming. Of course, besides being alert it helps to have West's great reflexes to make a play like that.

15. I don't get angry because I've got to stay in control, keep my cool. But I get close to angry when my man scores on me. So that's my motivation for defense. I take my man's basket personally. I can play passive defense until he starts scoring. Then I start picking him up right away to show him that I'm the man. But, like in the 1972 playoffs, I was really into defense against Jerry West. During the season I didn't play that well against him. I was reaching too much, that's a problem I have. I'd be slapping him as he was going up to shoot or when he was trying to drive. Not enough footwork by me. So now I was out to prove that I could stop him, that I could get it up on defense. At this time West was not hitting too well. But I play West close all the time anyway because I don't want him to start hitting, and all he might need is one basket to get going.

16. Sometimes I take a rest on defense. But I don't mean that I doze. Usually I play an aggressive style, ready for a steal. But since I play 45 or so minutes of offense and defense, I've got to pace myself. I do it on offense when I kick the ball off to whoever might be hot at the moment. On defense I play my man but I'm not wasting a lot of effort. I ease out of the play at certain times, relax, but just to make sure my man doesn't get the ball. I'm not setting up for a steal. I'm just playing a good conservative defense.

17. Any guy who always turns his back to the ball on defense is a bad defensive player, and that's the guy you always work back-door on because he never knows where the ball is. He's always looking around. He'll be looking for the ball and his man is gone.

18. Shooting range. You want to keep a guy out of his shooting range if you can. Watch your man and see where he's comfortable shooting from. Most guys, it's about 20 feet or 25 feet maximum. So try to push them a few steps back, whether they have the ball or not. That makes a big difference, and he'll have to kind of force his shot. Get him back by crowding him. Come up and meet him. Try to catch him between dribbles so that he can't beat you by going around you.

Pete Maravich drives against Bill Bradley

Fronting in the pivot

19. Don't jump unless you think you have a good chance of blocking a shot, until the offensive man has committed himself or taken a shot. Then you should try to get a hand in his face. Other than that, like if he fakes and fakes, you should always try to stay on your feet and not go for the fake. If you do go for the fake, keep your hand high as you come down from the jump. Most guys who are good jumpers are prone to go off their feet a lot. They try to excel on blocking shots. They should try to play a good position rather than leaving their feet. Guys like Freddie Carter and Dave Bing and John Havlicek can really sky, so they try to block a lot of shots. If a guy's right-handed and you force him left, when he stops to shoot he's got to bring the ball up in your face, so you've got a good chance to block the shot or distract him.

20. To block a shot, don't lunge. Go straight up. Don't swing at the ball. Don't follow through, don't break your wrist or a foul might be called. At times you can jump around your man and block the shot from the rear, but that's a risk. Then you can't block him out if he gets the shot off. When a man is driving in, and if you feel you have a chance to block the shot without fouling him, I think it's a good move. But normally if the guy has a good inside position on you it has to be a great defensive play to block the shot.

21. After a man shoots a jump-shot from about 30 feet or closer, I try to block him out. But that's a lost art. Hardly anybody blocks out that well anymore. I find in the pros that guys don't block out, especially on the Knicks. Certain guards you know go to the boards to follow their shot more than others. Guys like Freddie Carter and Bing, and Jerry Sloan. You use your body to block him out. You spin around after he shoots and you sort of spread out. Get a wide stance and stretch your arms, your body on his legs. But you can't hold him back, can't cup a guy with your hands. But you got him. The only thing he can do is run right over your back.

In college we blocked out a lot because we had a small team. We had to block out because we didn't have guys who were good jumpers. In the pros, guys don't feel a need to block out, which isn't right. That's how I get a lot of rebounds. Norm Van Lier of the Bulls does, too. Nobody ever blocks us out. I'm just hanging around the basket. And they forget about me. Once I shoot or somebody else shoots, they turn their heads. In the pros everybody stands at the basket, and that way I've got a good chance of getting the rebound. Whereas if you block out, and you're on the inside, you should get that rebound.

Like the tip over Chamberlain I made in the 1972 Laker playoffs. Nobody blocked me out. Everybody just followed the ball, so I was in a position to tap it in.

Even those rare guys who do block out, they'll do it only on their man. But they're not about to block out anybody else. They figure that if it's not their man it doesn't matter. I think you should block a man out whether he's a guard or forward or center.

22. I keep mental notes on guys. If I'm guarding a guy, right away his game, what he likes to do, flashes back to me. Some guys keep a written book, like Cazzie Russell. I don't have to write in a book. I *live* the book.

23. Someone should always be back to protect against the fast break, and that is usually me for the Knicks. I lay back when I don't have the ball, so I do what they call "balancing the court." I get in the center of the court in case the other team is going to try to burn us on the break. Some guys don't get in the center. They'll run down the side of the court and look to hit the offensive boards. They won't give much consideration to who's back. There are a lot of times I feel I could go to the board and get the rebound. But if I went, who's going to protect back?

Nate Archibald makes a move on Kareem Abdul-Jabbar

Norm Van Lier lets the seed fly.

I think Dick Barnett is trying to tell somebody something, as Jeff Mullins drives.

Siding in the pivot.

24. Some guys never make the change from offense to defense. When I make a bad pass and the other team gets the ball, in my mind's eye I'm asking myself why I threw the pass. And I'm telling myself not to do it again, like maybe I made a lob instead of a bounce pass. Or I left my feet. Just a quick thought while I'm running back on defense. Now I'm on defense. When I'm on offense, I'm all offense. But when we lose the ball, I'm all defense. I'm getting back to my man. Some guys, if they make a bad pass, stand there arguing about the pass and throwing their hands up in disgust, like maybe they're blaming a teammate for not being where they threw it. Meanwhile you can be beating them on the fast-break.

These are some of the things I think about when I'm . . . Guarding the NBA's Best Guards

LENNIE WILKENS, Cleveland: He's one of those guards who's quicker than me, so I give him an extra step. I mean, I may be three or four steps away from him, instead of two—whatever you have to do to compensate for his speed. You can't crowd him. Lennie is all left. The problem is keeping him to his right. I give him that whole right side. He tries to suck you in, fake and come back. But I don't go for that. I just stay in my same position, giving him a lot of room. Lennie's not that good of an outside shot, so I drop off him, maybe give him a shot. But there are very few guys you can do that to. Most guys are good quick shooters. And when I say lay off an extra step or so, that's only if they are out of shooting range. If they are at the top of the circle I can't step back. I have to get up on them. Otherwise they shoot.

Lennie basically looks for the drive. And he looks for picks. So you got to get over the pick. Talking and helping out, that comes with team defense. This takes him out of the pattern because his main thing is driving. He'll fake right one or two dribbles, then quick he'll come back left. Even though I know all this, know his moves, a lot of times I still can't stop him.

GAIL GOODRICH, Los Angeles: Also a lefty, and fast. But not quite as fast as Wilkens. A better shot. I have to stay closer on him. Like a Bill Bradley, can't leave him open.

CALVIN MURPHY, Houston: Right-handed. Fast. Good shot. Force him left. Give him that extra step because he can go around you.

NATE ARCHIBALD, KC-Omaha: Presents a big problem. He's a great ball-handler. Unselfish. No one man can stop him. He has to be double-teamed. A very effective driver, so you need help from your center. Try to make him give the ball up. He's lefty. Otherwise I play him same way as Murphy.

The thing about playing against smaller guards like Goodrich, Murphy and Archibald is to put the pressure on them. I know they can't stop me if I'm backing in and get off a good shot. That has a psychological effect on them. But if they keep scoring on me, it's the reverse. The pressure's on me. If I score against them I think the coach will have to take them out because they have to get somebody in that can stop you.

JEFF MULLINS, Golden State: He's got great offense, good outside shot. He uses picks a lot. Guarding him is like playing in a forest.

DAVE BING, Detroit: He's both ways, can shoot outside and drives great. He loves the corners. Right-handed. Try to force him out of the corners and to his left. Great leaper, so I try to keep him outside, too.

ARCHIE CLARK, Bullets: He likes to use the crossover dribble—takes you right and then switches to left. I try to force him to his right. I'm close enough so that he can't crossover dribble. In this case I'm forcing a man right who is right-handed, which might seem like an exception to my rule of sending a man to his weakness. But his strength is the crossover, so by stopping that I found I could contain him. Especially on the fast-break. Whereas instead of dropping back, I picked him up as soon as I could wherever I thought I could without him going around me. So like I minimize his speed, make him slow down a bit and then overplay him for the crossover dribble.

I watch Calvin Murphy grow.

Archie Clark looks for daylight.

DeBusschere (22) and Jo Jo White under the boards—also known as "the butcher shop."

EW YORK
22
ELTICS

OSCAR ROBERTSON, Milwaukee: Dick Barnett said that if you give Oscar a 12-foot shot, he'll work on you until he's a got a 10-foot shot. Give him 10, he wants 8. Give him 8, he wants 6. Give him 6, he wants 4. Give him 4, he wants 2. Give him 2, you know what he wants? That's right, baby. A layup.

Oscar is great, though he is getting old and slowing down a little. He's got a jump-shot that you can't stop because of his timing and because he holds it so far back over his head. But usually he's going to jockey you for position. He's going to back you in and try to use his weight so that he's playing one-on-one. He's not going to beat you with quickness. He dares you to stop him. He's going to use a very simple move where he just takes you down and tries to get you to jump, or he can jump into you, or just fake and you don't go up and he just goes up to shoot.

With Oscar, I got to use body contact because he's going to know where I am anyway, and because he's going to bump into me if I don't bump into him. I don't slap at the ball because he controls it too well. And I don't keep dropping back, so you have to try to force him away from the basket. It's more like guarding the center, you know, whereas you keep bouncing him, trying to force him farther out.

JERRY WEST, Los Angeles: West is quicker than Robertson and shoots from farther out. But he can drive great, too. Right-handed. I give West an extra step and try to force him left. He is good going either way, but maybe if he goes left I have a fraction of a percentage working for me. You can never completely stop a great player like West. You just try to keep him below his average. He has a quick release. I try to keep my hand in his face. I used to try to steal the ball too much from him. I'd lunge and get careless. And I got called for fouls. I put pressure on myself. I pray a lot when I guard him.

NORM VAN LIER, Chicago: He's all hustle. He hangs around the basket. I concentrate on

Jerry Lucas works to get free in the pivot, guarded by John Havlicek. Willis Reed looks to give him pass. Dave Cowens defends against Reed.

REED
19
18

keeping him outside and always remember to block him out after he shoots.

JO JO WHITE, Boston: A good long-range shooter. He doesn't drive that much but he can. He's quick, right-handed. Send him to his left because he likes to dribble right-handed.

BOB WEISS, Chicago: He used to give me a lot of trouble. Still does, but recently I've been handling him pretty good. But I got tired of people saying that Weiss had my number. He's lefty and fast and he got points off me. I've been having greater success making him go right and stay right. Before, I would force him right and then let him come back left. I was being too relaxed. And he had some good games against the Knicks. Like once he had 10 points in the first half. Most of it wasn't my fault because he got several fast-break layups. So at halftime our coach, Red Holzman, he looks at the stat sheet and says, "Clyde, you better get on this guy, he's got 10 points already!"

EARL MONROE is on the Knicks now, and the best thing about it is that I don't have to guard him anymore. But I tried to play him straight up, not overplaying him either way. You know he likes to back in all the time, spin moves and all that stuff, so you let him make a move and then you react.

Pearl, he makes those twitches and darts and you don't like him showing on you, making a fancy basket off a spin move with the crowd screaming. He likes to leave you hanging in the air from a fake. There were times I'd reach for the ball and he'd be up shooting. Next time I'd say, "Clyde, wait, don't reach for it," and he'd drive past me. And he could make a basket without looking, that's how it seemed. I figure he was shooting best when I was all over him. Then I'd get back and he'd hit for another 2 points. It drove me wild. But nobody could keep that up, not even Monroe. You just keep working on a guy. Pretty soon he's got to be affected. You hope.

Bob Cousy, great passer.

PETE MARAVICH, Atlanta: You try to get him angry at himself, so you pressure him. If he makes a bad pass or you steal it from him you might be able to break downcourt for an easy layup because he's at the other end talking to himself. And with his hair flying, you sort of wait for him to stop dribbling. Then for a second all the hair that's been flying in the wind comes down over his face and he can't see. That's when you steal the ball. He can make the most incredible shots. When he's hot, you just have to wait until the hurricane lets up.

CHARLIE SCOTT, Phoenix: He does everything wrong. Like he always leaves his feet. But he's able to hang up there long enough to either shoot or until somebody comes open. He does a lot of ad-libbing in the air. He likes to come down on the semi-fast-break and give you some head fakes and go around you, so I've got to honor his first move. I've got to retreat when he's beyond the key. He's a righty, so I try to angle him so that he has to go left, to flare out. He jumps so high you can hardly block his shot. But when he shoots going left he keeps the ball low and sometimes I'll have a chance to deflect it.

GEOFF PETRIE, Portland: Great outside shooter. Maybe he and West have the best range. Nice touch. He burned me in the first half of a game early in the 1972 season. He used picks on me to go back-door. I was lazy. I was just watching him and not seeing the ball. When he went away from the ball I relaxed. I thought I was guarding him but I wasn't. After his third back-door basket I started watching the ball, too, and playing him tighter. The clamps closed on him.

AUSTIN CARR, Cleveland: A lot like Petrie. Accurate from 25 or 30 feet. Got to hustle. His team sets a lot of picks for him.

LOU HUDSON, Atlanta: Tough coming off the pick. Not a natural guard, so isn't that great a ball-handler. I've had success sending him to his left.

JIMMY WALKER, Houston: Likes to maneuver off the dribble. Can shoot deep. Doesn't drive much. He'll settle for pulling up. Try to crowd him.

Team defense comes in against guys like Nate and Pete. Because anytime you get someone turning his back or dribbling a lot you should usually make a steal. Earl Monroe helps me a lot and sometimes we're able to take it away.

I'm one of the few guards who doesn't mind getting switched onto forwards. Most forwards are happy to have a smaller man, a guard, accidentally get on them. They all try to overpower you and they get careless. I think I can take the ball away from them. I'm so quick I hardly let them take a dribble. They bounce once and I'm gone with it.

Havlicek is one of the toughest forwards because he can control the ball well. He shoots good from outside so you've got to really get up on him. Don't anticipate, because I think he's toughest when he's coming down on the break, when he's got speed, he gives you fakes and goes to the basket. It's a challenge. You got to match his quickness with your quickness. Better man wins.

But you could get caught on anybody. By the same token, they could get caught on me.

Of course, you don't usually get too excited when you have to switch onto a Chamberlain, an Abdul-Jabbar, a Spencer Haywood, or a Thurmond. But you play them basically the same as you play anyone else. Force them to their weakness.

What I try to do is force him in back of me under the basket. And if he likes to hook right-handed then I try to force him to go left-handed. A Chamberlain, you try to force him to his right, then he usually won't shoot, even though he's right-handed. He likes to come back for the dipper move, you know, roll it off his right hand but going to his left. Very seldom does he dip coming from the right side.

With Abdul-Jabbar I'm in trouble because he can maneuver both ways so only thing I can do there is try to keep him away from the basket. Belly him, you know, move around and bounce on him like a fat crab.

If a guy's on the low post, like Spencer Haywood plays, you usually have to stay behind him. But if a guy moves up higher, or if he's about your size, you can front him. But you don't front him if he's going to roll to the basket for a lob pass.

So then you have to play him on the side where the ball is, with your arm out, so he's having trouble getting a pass into him.

Team Defense

The Knicks have made team defense famous. And all it involves is all the individual basics I've talked about, with maybe the most important thing being reacting to the ball. Like if a ball goes to the corner man, the defensive forward goes out to get him, the defensive guard slides over, the other defensive guard slides over to take the first guard's place, the center stays where he is, but the other forward moves up to cover the offensive guard closest to him. (See Diagram 1.)

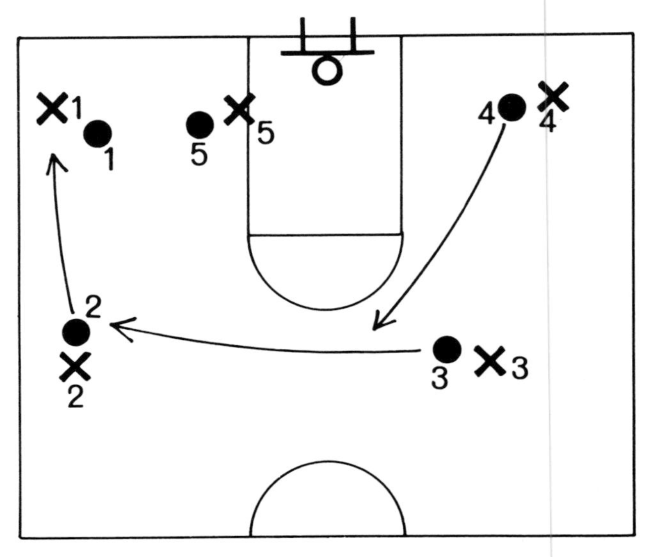

Double-teaming. X1 has the ball, guarded by circle 1. Everyone except circle 5 shifts. X4 is left free, but he could only get the ball on a dangerous cross-court pass.

Freddie (Mad Dog) Carter leaps at Austin Carr fake.

CELTICS
10
NEW YORK
15
COWENS
18

YORK
17

Dave Bing goes up against Bob Dandridge. Bing keeps wrist stiff in order to avoid fouling.

Blocking out for rebound

So one offensive guy is left free because now the defensive guard and forward are double-teaming the man in the corner. But the guy who is free is on the other side of the court. To get the ball to him there's got to be a cross-court pass. And we can pick that off.

Team defense is adjusting to the situation. And it's working in complete harmony. It's five guys working as one. It would be like the pistons in my Rolls. Everything moving smooth, man, every guy adjusting, sliding forward and back depending on the situation.

Talking comes with team defense. You need a lot of talking—screaming—for things like picks-and-rolls, a basic play of basketball that works most of the time if the defense doesn't talk. Like San Francisco. Jeff Mullins and Nate Thurmond use it a lot. Nate sets a pick for Jeff. I try to bust through and Nate spins for the basket. Say Willis is guarding Nate. Willis has been trying to help me with Jeff. So Willis got to get back fast if Nate cuts for the basket. If Willis can't I got to switch on Nate. That's trouble. Nate is 7 inches taller than me.

The back man especially, that would be Willis in this case, has to talk. He has to tell the back man to step up and go over the pick. By going over the pick, I mean you slide or step in front of the man picking you off to get to the man you're guarding. When the man you're guarding is setting a pick, call it out to your teammate. You got to scream it out so that everybody in the place can hear you when you see a teammate being set up for a pick. I almost got killed a couple years ago on a pick by Van Lier. My hip hit his knee and I went down like I was shot. At the last moment I heard "pick"—like a whisper. Scream it, "PICK RIGHT!"

Defensing the Fast-break

If there are two men back—with three offensive men coming at you—you play similar to a zone. When the ball is in the corner, the back man goes out to get the ball and the middle man drops back to protect the basket. When the ball is in the middle, the top man's job is to stop the penetration of the guy.

What I try to do—rather than guarding the man bringing the ball down on a fast break—is to play the middle man straight up. As I see him approaching me, I either send him to his left or to his right. So again I've taken away an alternative. He can only go one way. So if I'm the top man I'll force the guy to his left if he's right-handed, and vice versa.

Rebounding

I put this in the defense section because I think that the inside man, which is the defensive man (he's supposed to be closer to the basket because he's supposed to be protecting it), should normally get the rebound. If you block out. But if you don't block out, then the offensive player has an equal chance of getting the board, sometimes even a better chance, because he can jump higher. He's got a running start. You're just standing there.

I'm blocking you out about 5 or 6 feet from the basket or farther. It depends on the rim. If it's lively, a ball will bounce deep. You have to know that. So there are a lot of deep rebounds, and that's when the guards have to help out. You've got to test the rims before a game to find out if they're dead or alive.

Rebounding is position and timing. If I've got good position on a man, blocking him out right, it doesn't usually matter how much taller he is. I should get the rebound, because I'm in front of him, unless he pushes me or climbs over me—in other words, fouls me.

Rebounding is like good defense. You got to move your feet to block the man out. Then you meet the ball at the top of your jump with your arms fully extended.

A lot of rebounding is instinct and experience. I can pretty much tell where the ball is going to bounce. I think it's something you're born with, like quick hands. And many times rebounding has nothing to do with leaping, because some guys

NEW YORK
22
NEW
24
10
3

I know there's a ball there somewhere.

can jump to the moon but they can't rebound. They don't have the timing. When the ball hits the rim they're going up, and now the ball's coming off and they're coming down.

A lot of guys in the pros can't rebound. Like Cazzie Russell. He's a great shot, but not much of a rebounder. He's always jumping on a different plane from the ball. The ball's going up, he's coming down, and vice versa.

I'm not a great jumper, but I'm a good rebounder. I'm one of the top rebounding guards in the league. What I like most on the rebound is hanging a long time, waiting on the ball and knowing when I should go up for it—the exact moment.

I usually rebound with two hands if I can, but sometimes you got to go up with one. If I'm in a crowd, I want to rebound two-handed, draw the ball into my chest, elbows out protecting the ball. But if there's just one guy behind me I rebound one-handed. In this way you can come off dribbling right away. Rebound, snatch and whiz away.

When it's the other way, when a guy gets the rebound on me and tries to dribble in a crowd, I can knock the ball away from him. So I come down and protect the ball first, then see where everybody is before I make a move. Check it out and see what's happening.

Sometimes you may not be able to grab the ball off the board. But you can get finger tips on it. So try to tap the ball back up. Keep the ball in play. Maybe one of your teammates can come up with a rebound. Or maybe you'll get a second chance or a third chance at it.

Stealing: a Detail

When I was ten years old, my friend and I went into the backyard of the "haunted house" in our neighborhood in Atlanta. We snuck in to steal pecans that had fallen off the tree. All of a sudden this old man comes out with a gun and starts shooting at us. We ran. I was so scared I was running without touching the ground. My friend was actually slightly wounded. The man was brought to trial. I don't remember what happened to him. All I remember was the fright. That was the last time I stole anything outside of the basketball court.

Funny thing, stealing is the part of the game I love best. Stealing a ball and then scoring the basket, or passing for the score. Stealing is a calculated gamble. I don't think you can be conservative and make steals. You got to gamble to a certain extent. But you can look foolish if you lose. It's like a card player. You're watching what the other guy does. As the game goes on you know what the guy would bet on, right? And like you try to sucker him with different hands, try to make him show his hand, you know. Stealing a basketball is about the same. Anticipation and quickness and cool.

There are three times to make a steal: off a dribble, off a pass and straight out of a man's hands when he's holding the ball.

I find that most kids relax a lot on defense. So your man comes up with the ball, bang, he makes the basket. It only looks like I'm relaxing on defense. But I'm playing possum. That's my way of suckering a guy in. But I always know where the ball is, and I always know where the man is. That's one reason why I make a lot of steals. Your man might be careless when he sees you looking relaxed. I find that if you crowd guys all the time it's very difficult to make a steal. They're aware that you're there.

What I do then is what I call lulling my man to sleep. But I'm watching his habits, getting the rhythm of the cadence of his dribble. Everyone has a certain rhythm that he dribbles to. I spend a lot of the game waiting for a guy to make a mistake. But not to the point that when I try for the steal I'm out of position if I miss the ball. I'm still in good position because I'm not lunging for the ball. I'm just reaching with my hands, like a flick. I can try to steal the ball but still be in front of a man. Because I usually only try to steal if the dribbler has the ball in front of me.

The good players don't get careless with the ball that often, but everybody gets careless sometimes. You wait maybe all game for that one moment. But I find that in the last five minutes of the game there's a lot of pressure and some guys get careless. This is the time when I try to capitalize. Before, the guy, if he's good—if he's West or Robertson or Clark—is dribbling low and with the ball protected between him and me, protecting the ball with his body. Now he might start to dribble higher because he's really involved in the game and I haven't been pressuring him all that much. I'm away two, three steps. He's kind of conditioned to my giving him room.

In the last game of the championship playoffs against the Lakers in 1970, I was guarding Dick Garrett. I gave him room to breathe, let him get a little careless. By the third quarter he had the ball right out in front of him and was hardly thinking I was in the gym. There were times I knew I could take it from him, but didn't. I was waiting for the best time to demoralize the team. So I was following the cadence of his dribble. One-two-three dribbles, then shoot. I was taking all this down in my head. In the third quarter there was a moment when I said, "Clyde, that's the end of playin' possum. Get it!" And it was curtains.

I only try to steal the ball off the dribble at certain times in the game, and usually at certain points on the court. The best zones for stealing are at half-court and along the sidelines. If I miss the ball the dribbler might backtrack and get a backcourt violation called against him. And if I miss it on the sidelines he still doesn't have room to do much—not like if he's in the middle of the floor.

When I steal it, I steal with a flick, a straight jab. You're following the cadence, and as soon as he goes through the next bounce—immediately when it leaves his hand—that's when I go, not with the ball on the way up but on the way down. What I notice about my steals, just messing around like with the kids at Kutsher's camp, is that it's very soft. It's not a bang. I steal with a soft touch, like a classy pickpocket.

Sometimes I can knock the ball away by reaching from behind. That's part of the possum theme. You sucker a guy into thinking he's breezed by you. And sometimes I'll try to knock the ball from behind. But only when he's on the strong side, when I've got teammates who can cover my gamble. On the weak side (when there's only two of us Knicks), the guy could be past for an easy layup. It's also not normally a good play, because my chances of fouling increase since I'm usually lunging instead of reaching with balance.

Most of the time I steal a ball it's not my man I steal it from. I steal it from behind a pick or screen. You're almost hiding behind a tree and then dart out—with perfect timing. One of my favorite steals was on Jerry West in the last game of the 1970 playoffs. It's rare to steal off West. I was guarding Garrett and Mike Riordan was guarding West at about midcourt. West faked toward the middle then started dribbling hard to his left. He didn't see me but I was watching him out of the corner of my eye. I edged away from my man, streaked in front of West and took off with the ball.

That wasn't exactly what I meant by stealing off a pick or screen. In those cases, you go around a defensive man who has intentionally tried to block you off from the man you're guarding. But that West steal was one of the coolest I ever made, so I don't mind mentioning it.

On plays like that, I'm really out of position. But the trick is to catch me out of position, like I'm gambling on a particular play. So guys might just wait and make me commit myself and they could hit my man with a pass. But I usually outsmart them.

You're watching everything all the time. You know where everybody is on the court. And you keep track of what certain players like to do. Some guys like to make crossover dribbles or cross-court passes, some guys like to make lob passes. I might be watching, say, Lucius Allen, the

CELTIC
7
YORK
0
CELTICS
16

Bucks' guard. Maybe he gets the ball on the side and lobs it in to the center, Kareem Abdul-Jabbar. I might be on the other side of the free-throw line, away from the action. So now we start pressuring on defense. Allen is forced out a little higher but is still making the same pass. I'm watching this all game. Now my man is on the strong side, in the low post. I don't usually have to worry about him because the concentration is on Abdul-Jabbar. So I wait for the lob pass. Abdul-Jabbar gets it, starts his fakes, worrying only about our center, who's guarding him. I sneak along the baseline. I gamble. I leave my man. I don't get burned that much because it's not that obvious. I don't let him see me coming, and if he does he has to do everything in his power to protect me from stealing the ball. So he can't just throw it to my man. If I can't knock the ball away, then I get back quick to my man. This is one trick that I often save for the end of the game. I might be able to make this steal earlier, but then if I do the center will guard against it. So I lay in wait until a crucial moment—and then turn the game around.

Another way to steal passes is what is called playing the passing lane. That's the lane where the ball will be traveling. I like to give my man room here, too. So does Jerry West. But as the game goes on, both of us sort of inch up until we're just laying for that unsuspecting pass.

A lot of it is instinct, too. sometimes you just have a feeling the ball will be coming in your direction. But you also look for things, like a guy's eyes. He might glance real fast where he's going to throw the ball. Or a guy calls a play and you've seen the play before. Or when your guys are double-teaming someone and he throws a pass to a man who does not go to meet the ball. So I go to meet it for him.

But you got to watch for the fake, when a guy is trying to outsmart you. The back-door play. The passer sees you edging up on your man, then fakes a pass and you're lunging and the man you're guarding goes to the basket for the pass and 2 points. I used to get burned on that a lot. I'm cooler now. All in being alert.

I make some easy steals after I score on a layup. Most guys will run back without seeing the ball. I make the layup and I never lose sight of the ball. Right away I play possum. I know where my man is. I might run like my back is to the ball, but right away I turn around. Lots of guys are careless when they pass the ball in. Especially the big men. Or it might be the guy I scored on. He might be thinking about me scoring on him and forget that he's on offense now.

But I'm looking out of the corner of my eye. Big men, a lot of times, have only one foot in-bounds rather than planting both feet. They're falling forward. They either have to step in-bounds or throw the ball.

I made that play in the first NBA-ABA all-star game and it was the basket that put us ahead for good. You just discover which guys do it. Like we had Nate Bowman. He was great for that. He'd just take the ball out, he'd never look, you know. One foot back. Some guys are notorious for that. They want to rush it in. I don't know why. It's an obsession with them. Some big guys are set and you don't try it with them. Like Wes Unseld of the Bullets. The guards are usually under control because they do that trick themselves. Jerry West is one of the best at it.

Another way to steal a ball is to knock it out of a guy's hands when he's holding it. I flick up. I don't bat down because the refs usually call that for some reason. It's timing, and I don't know how you develop it. But when you see a man holding the ball in front of you (or sneak up from behind a center, or a rebounder), and if you're quick enough, it should be yours.

I made a steal against Archie Clark in the 1971 playoffs that I can never remember making before. At least not under such pressure. It was the last game of the playoff series against Baltimore. The Bullets were ahead 97–95 with about 2 minutes to go in the last quarter. I'm guarding Clark, who's a good dribbler, can go with either hand. I'm close on him because the game's tight. He comes across the top of the key. I wasn't even thinking steal. I was just trying to stop him because he was hot. My idea was to get in front of him, cut him off. I did. Then he stops his dribble. I grabbed the ball right out of his hands. Bam, I was gone—so fast. I never knew how I did it. He stopped and I had the ball, that's all. I was in position and he made the mistake of not protecting the ball. I scampered downcourt—2 points. He's still standing there. Tie game.

Now the pressure's on them, pressure's on Archie. The crowd is screaming. next time Archie gets the ball I'm all over him. He's lost the ball once, now he's going to try to redeem himself, try to beat me. I pick him up right away. He's a little shaky now. He makes another mistake. Again I get the ball, score. We go ahead and win.

That's my whole psychology in the last minutes. Pressure him. But it all depends on how I feel. If I feel I can go strong for the last five minutes, I'll do it. But if I think I'll tire after two, I'll wait. Maybe I put it on too soon—like in the first period. I used to do that when I was younger. I didn't have the experience of pacing myself. I'd get so psyched up I couldn't stay away from the ball. I figured that whenever I was out there, it was time for my show. But I learned patience. Like the good gambler. You wait, you watch, then you make off with the whole pot.

NEW YORK
10

Offense:

"Making a Poem"

When I'm coming down with the ball I usually don't know what's going to happen when I cross the half-court line. I don't make up my mind that I'm going to shoot, I'm going to pass . . . I just go. Whatever happens happens. I don't mean that we're running around like Keystone Kops. The Knicks have about five basic plays that we use, but even there we've got options and alternatives for them. We have our fundamentals, our fakes and cuts and picks and we're working together to get a man open for a jump-shot or spring a guy loose for a drive.

It's like making up something—making a poem or something. You're coming down, playing around. With words it's the same thing. You're in control, you know what the goal is and you're not sure how you're going to get there. But you're pretty sure you will, and it's going to be exciting. That's one of the joys of basketball—improvising.

It's almost impossible to practice moves because most moves professional guys make are moves that are instinct. They are made up on the spur of the moment. Like I could teach you the behind-the-back dribble, the crossover dribble. I could teach you those. Those are basic moves. But as far as faking up and drawing a 3-point play or something, I can show you how to do that, but you might not have the timing to carry it out. You might have the problem that when you fake up you'd never be set to shoot. You'd fake too hard. That was the problem I had. It was a wasted fake because when the guy went up I wasn't ready to jump. So now when he came down I was trying to shoot around him, taking a bad shot.

The amazing thing about making a move is that I might never have made it before and I might never make it again. It's just happening. I can remember moves in playoffs that amazed me. I remember one beautiful move I made against the Lakers in the 1972 playoffs. I was driving down the baseline for the basket. I left my feet, which I shouldn't have done because I could have lost control. I was actually looking for someone to pass to. Jim McMillian and Happy Hairston, I think, were on me. So to avoid them I brought the ball down. That was my first pump and I went by these two guys, pumping, and I just came around and up on the other side of the basket for a perfect two-handed layup.

Another thing about offense is, I make the move and see how you guard it. I make one move and you react one way and I say, "God, I had the shot. I could have got the shot off." So the next time I might make the same move and go through the same motions and maybe you'll do the same thing and I'll take the shot. I might dribble baseline and fake like I'm coming back to the middle and I'll notice I could have gone all the way along the baseline. The next time I'll try to drive baseline. The same way on defense. If I'm guarding a guy I could say to myself, "Wow, I could have stolen the ball." So the next time you come down I'll do the same thing and see what happens.

Now there was another move that I studied. I watched the films and saw how West was doing a good job on me. He gambles a lot and reaches around because there's Chamberlain. If you drive past West, there's Chamberlain. So West sometimes lets you get past him. And you usually can't drive because of Chamberlain, so you pull up for a jump-shot and West is *behind* you to block the shot. So what I did was drive past him fast and then slow my dribble as though I was going to shoot. Now West commits himself. Then I take a few more dribbles in right quick and shoot the jump-shot. I've left West behind.

Offense is where a lot of guys like to show, doing all kinds of fancy stuff which isn't necessary. All that between the legs, all that spinning and turning, all that hipper-dipper. For what? Unless you're on Earl Monroe it's just wasting a lot of energy and going nowhere and slowing the game up. And there's only one Pearl, man. Otherwise it ruins your game and the team's game. The other guys start standing around, cooling off and getting resentful.

I use fancy stuff only when I have to, when it's necessary. My theory is if it helps you score, if you can get a step on your man, then it's a good move. If you go behind-your-back and the guy's still on you, then it was a wasted motion. So I try to waste as few motions as I can. Everything I do on offense is designed to get me open or one of my teammates open for a basket.

When we have Willis Reed in the center, a close-in threat to score, passing becomes my primary offense. And I actually rest a lot so I can go full steam on defense. On offense if somebody else has a hot hand, I constantly lay the ball on him, whereas a lot of guys just—you know, everybody's scoring, so they figure, well, it's my turn. Only when I score two or three baskets in a row do I try to take over the offense for a while, you know, when I start to burn. Other than that I'll just move the seed around to somebody else who has the hot hand.

That has a lot to do with being an effective leader and playmaker. It's my responsibility as ball-handler to get the whole team wheeling and dealing. Willis says it's my ball and I just let the other guys play with it. Well, most guys don't care if that's true as long as they get their shots.

Improvising in the air.

Like Earl Monroe. He knew I was handling the ball at guard about 80 percent of the time, but he didn't complain because he was popping enough.

And I found when I was a rookie that if the big guys know you'll kick the ball off to them, they'll run downcourt a lot faster.

So a playmaker's big role is to keep harmony on offense. I think I did this in the 1973 playoffs, especially against the Lakers. I'm hip to the way Phil Jackson summed it up. Jackson said, "Clyde wasn't getting his points, so he just stayed in the back seat and guided us in."

Playmaking

I've seen guys make fancy passes that wow the crowd and bounce off the back of a teammate's head. That's not playmaking. And I've seen tricky guys dribble all over the court until everyone except the defense starts to fall asleep. That's not playmaking, either.

Playmaking is handling the ball, being under control, knowing where everybody on the court is and making the play—he passes the ball when he should and dribbles when he should and shoots when he should. But people like to watch somebody who's exciting, even if he's not that good.

A playmaker's just making a play that's there. Like the pick and roll. You can only do two things. If the play's there you make it, if not you hold the ball. If your man who set the pick doesn't get clear when he rolls toward the basket, then don't throw it. Otherwise that's trying to make a play that's not there. But if I run you off the pick and the back defensive man doesn't come up to play me, then I know I have a jump-shot. So it's important to know what's happening all the time on the court.

One of my problems is that sometimes I still try to force the pass. I'll throw it into a crowd, or sometimes you see Bradley and you try to run the back-door when he's going toward the basket and doesn't have a step on his man, and I'll try to bounce the ball to him when there's actually no play. Sometimes I see a man too late and I'll try to whip the ball on him. You see, the timing's off, and then I look up and I see a man's open but it's too late, it should have been a second before that second.

One of the playmaker's biggest jobs is assists. If a guy makes a basket off a pass from you, whether it's a layup or what, you should get an assist. To be a great assist man is the same as being a great playmaker. It's beautiful for me to make a great pass to a guy who makes a nice basket. It's like a quarterback. He doesn't score the touchdown, but he knows he's had a lot to do with it. It gives you a tingle. That's why after a game I usually look at the assists before anything else on the statistics sheet. When I broke the Knick career assist record in 1973, held by Dick McGuire, I was thrilled. Dick is a Knick scout now, and he was at the game. I joked with him afterward. I said, "Sorry about that, Dick." He said, "The only reason you broke the record was you had better shooters to pass to."

Another responsibility of a playmaker is to penetrate, to go into the lane and draw guys on you. Then you pass off to the open man. If you have a one-on-one situation you might be able to jump-shoot or drive. Unless the other one is a Nate Thurmond. Then the lane becomes what they call "Death Alley," or "The Avenue of Broken Dreams."

The penetrator should be able to pass off the dribble, so he must be a pretty good ball-handler. He has to keep his head up—otherwise, if he is double-teamed he'll get tied up with the ball. And he should always keep the ball low when he's dribbling into heavy traffic, like he usually does in the middle.

A playmaker's got to have the ball a lot, of course. And some teams need two basketballs. That's what the problem was when the Pistons had Dave Bing and Jimmy Walker. And that's

No. Try to keep it simple.

what people thought when Earl Monroe joined the Knicks. But it hasn't happened that way. I make sure Earl gets his hands on the ball enough so he can do his magic show.

The top assist guys—Wilkens, Oscar, Archibald—they've got to handle the ball a lot. But they are the best at it, and they know what to do with the ball better than anyone else. And like on the court Red Holzman will holler, "Give the ball to Clyde." He always wants me to be handling it because I start most of our plays.

Passing

1. You got to have control of the ball. If I don't have a good strong grip before I pass it, my ball will normally be intercepted or I'll throw the ball into the hands of the guy selling popcorn.

2. The great passers, like Oscar, throw soft but firm passes. Soft enough for the receiver to handle, quick enough for it to get there.

3. You should always make certain that the guy you're passing to is ready. If the ball is stolen it's always the passer's fault. Even if I hit a guy in the back, it's still the passer's fault because he threw the ball. If a guy's not looking, even though he should be looking it's still your fault. You should be in control and not throw the ball if it's not going to lead to something good. Just because the receiver is always supposed to be watching the ball doesn't mean he is. That's why guys have trouble with a Pistol Pete, because you never know where his passes are coming from. He's improving but he's still not consistent. One time it might be behind-the-back, the next over the head, the next off your head. Sometimes I'll pass the ball without looking, too. It's interesting. You might try to draw two men on you and then pass the ball. then all you can do is hope your man is ready.

4. Chest pass. Use fingertips. My hands are spread wide on the ball, thumbs in, elbows out. Step forward. Snap the ball. Hands follow through, like you're doing the breaststroke.

5. Don't snap the ball too hard. Some guys try to be Superman, especially when they're close to the receiver. You should only snap it hard as the guy can handle it without knocking him down.

6. One-handed pass, or baseball pass. Straight motion. Don't break your wrist. Let the ball roll off your fingers. Some guys will break their wrist and the ball dips like a curve ball. Or I've been open so many times and some guy would throw a pass almost all the way to the ceiling. So by the time it starts coming down, me and the five guys on defense are waiting for it like we're firemen with a net. So instead of drawing back and curving, I actually throw the ball from behind my ear like a quarterback. That way you can zip it out quick without wasting time. But most big guys, like centers, they will twirl it. Some draw back and try to palm the ball and throw it that way. You can't get the feeling of it. They throw it long. Just too far for a guy to reach. But Nate Thurmond is an exception. He throws it from behind his ear, fast and accurate.

7. Scoop pass. It's a good pass, all in one motion. You're dribbling and you see a man break clear and right off the dribble you throw it. It's a bang-bang play.

8. Bounce pass. Some bad passers make this a hard pass to catch, but it doesn't have to be, not if your pass is right. Some guys will bounce it too close to the guy cutting, or they'll bounce it too far. Most passes you'll usually want to hit a guy about chest-high. But not necessarily on the bounce pass when a guy's cutting like for a back-door play. The guy cutting should be leaning over to catch the pass. The lead pass should bounce one easy bounce over his knees and right into his hands. But some guys, they'll put a skid on the ball and it lands in the first row. Don't make a bounce pass if you can pass it straight. A straight pass is usually easier to handle.

9. Leading a man on a pass is not easy. It's all in judgment. If you can judge how far away a

Two-hand push pass.

guy is you can pass to him. You want to throw it so that he can catch the ball without breaking stride.

You can practice passing to a certain extent. You can practice being a quarterback. You can improve, but you might never be great at it. It's just a talent that some guys have. Everybody can't be a pitcher, no matter how long or hard they practice. I think there's a knack involved that is instinct and is unexplainable. But you can practice against a wall. You throw to different spots. And you can practice passing with teammates. Always trying to develop a good rhythm, a good feel. But practice doesn't mean that when a guy goes back-door you're going to be able to hit him with the pass. A game situation is different. Like I've seen guys make fifty-straight free throws in practice, but in a game, in the last minute, when they need to make it, they can't. But they can practice a lot of free throws.

10. Behind-the-back. I seldom use it unless I can get it to a guy who's all alone and I can jive up the game a little at the same time. It's not as cool as it looks because it's not as sure as it should be. I'm actually pretty accurate with a right-hand behind-the-back, but not the left.

11. Catching the pass. Hands relaxed, not stiff. Catch it in your fingertips, not in your palms. Everything in basketball is mostly fingertips. You pass with fingertips, you dribble with fingertips, you shoot with fingertips. Watch the ball. Otherwise you might get a bloody nose. Some guys take their eye off the ball and start dribbling or passing or shooting before they really have it. And don't turn your back on the ball. Always know where it is.

Dribbling

To me the dribbling stance is a lot like defense.

1. Your weight is evenly distributed.

2. You're in a staggered stance, with knees and back bent.

3. Head up. You should not have to look at the ball. The feel should be comfortable. It should be sure, like scratching your nose in the dark.

4. Slide. You never cross your feet when you dribble per se unless you're really running with the ball.

5. Use fingertips, not your palm. Dribblers that kids should watch are Oscar Robertson and Jerry West. But kids don't like their dribbling style too much because it's fundamental. Kids prefer to copy somone who is tricky with the ball. Like we used to say in high school, this guy can really tap the ball. Now, a Robertson never goes behind his back, but he's a complete player, with straight fundamentals. He does everything like it should be done. But kids want to pattern after a Monroe with a spin or Clark with a crossover dribble, or even myself with a behind-the-back dribble. This is what kids like. They'll be trying to go between their legs before they can even dribble forward. The reason Oscar is so great is that he's dependable. He always has control of the ball in a key situation. He won't lose the ball, whereas with some others it's a gamble because their dribbling is shaky. They make fantastic plays but they might kick the ball away or throw it away.

6. Push the ball, don't slap at it.

7. Learn to dribble with either hand. Most kids can dribble right if they're righty and left if they're lefty, but they don't try to develop their weaker hand. Like making layups right-handed and left-handed. They hate to use the other hand. If you only go one way, you'll be a dead if the guy guarding you is not blind and doesn't have three feet. But the only way to acquire that skill is to practice. You can strengthen your other (weaker) hand. I lift weights and squeeze a rubber ball. You could also use your fingertips when you do push-ups.

8. When the man is guarding you, you should protect the ball with your body while dribbling. Keep your body between him and the ball.

Two-hand lead bounce pass.

Top: The baseball pass. Below: Wes Unseld, one of the best at the fast, baseball outlet pass, winds up against Jerry Lucas (far right) and Phil Jackson.

Demonstrating the two-hand bounce pass at Kutsher's basketball academy.

9. Keeping low. You should dribble about knee-high or a little higher. You can practice this by letting a little air out of your ball so that is doesn't bounce as high. You could maybe let out two pounds of a standard nine-pound ball.

10. Practice on a level surface because that's where you'll be playing. I learned to dribble in a bumpy, rocky schoolyard in Atlanta. And I think this was pretty good experience because if you can learn to control a ball that keeps bouncing every which way, you should be able to control it on a board floor. But now I practice only on level surfaces.

11. The only time I dribble high (belt- to chest-high) is when I'm fast-breaking. That's for speed. I throw the ball about a yard-and-a-half away from me when I start to fast-break so that I get some momentum. If I throw it out any farther it becomes a foot race between me and the other guy for the ball.

Red Holzman in his two-hand set shot days with the Rochester Royals.

12. I use the behind-the-back dribble only in an emergency. My coaches in high school and college didn't go for it, thought it was hot-doggin'. But I find it can be effective when a guy is playing you too close, leaning, and then I can put it behind my back to get a step on him. I still don't know how me or anyone else can do it without palming the ball. I guess it's mostly instinct. But a lot of guys go behind-the-back and lose the sight or feel of the ball for a second. You lose your step advantage when you're looking for the ball, and whatever good the play might have done doesn't do it anymore.

Making the behind-the-back dribble is all in the angle—your ball is away from your body and feet. You can't dribble behind your back standing straight up. So you've got to twist or bend your body at a slight angle and give the ball a sort of whip motion.

Shooting

Everyone shoots the way he has to, the way that is most natural. Cazzie Russell shoots a bullet, Bill Bradley shoots with a little arc, Jerry Lucas shoots a rocket launch and the ball starts soaring straight up like it has no destination. I shoot on a line when I'm alone, with an arc when there's some cat climbing my chest. But all of us learned solid fundamentals when we were young. When we got bigger and better we learned to jive up our styles. Usually we had to—or we wouldn't get the shot off.

Except for shots off the drive, the jump-shot is the only shot I shoot, the only shot I've ever known. Basketball has become such a fast game, and the guys are so big and quick, that the jump-shot is the only realistic shot you can normally take.

Red Holzman was a good guard in the days of two-hand shots. He's still a great shot. He can beat you just shooting from the center of the court, two-handed. But there's no speed in that

Then I come over and throw a pick for him.

The Give-and-Go
I pass to a teammate.

shot. I guarded Red in a practice to prove the point that he couldn't get the shot off. I could anticipate when he was getting ready to shoot, so he couldn't get the ball away.

A kid starting out today has to be able to shoot the jump-shot. You see some strange-looking jump-shots. As many kids as there are, you see almost as many different jump-shots. But my philosophy on that is, even if it looks like the kid is shooting wrong, if the ball goes in why change it? Take a guy like Dick Barnett. He shoots kicking his legs under him and it looks like he's twisting all out of shape. But his fundamentals are right and his ball locates the hole. He was lucky nobody changed him. But there was also this big guy who played with Detroit. He would sort of

I hesitate, then cut for the basket, get a lead pass.

get all knotted up and twirl the ball out of his hand. He was a terrible shooter. He was unlucky that nobody changed him.

When I first came up to the Knicks, I didn't think I would be much of an offensive player. It wasn't like college. I didn't know where they grew guys so big who were so quick.

I found I had two main problems: No. 1 was, when to take the shot. It wasn't that I couldn't make the shots. I could take the shots or I could pass off, but knowing which to do was the problem. I passed when I should have shot and shot when I should have passed. I looked bad. It was embarrassing.

And I was so nervous I was playing shaky. I was blowing the easiest layups. And from outside, if I

Connie Hawkins on a hipper-dipper. Dave DeBusschere defends.

missed the first shot I didn't shoot again. One miss and my confidence was crushed.

Then halfway through that first season, it was like everything happened overnight. I was like suppressed dynamite, to use Cal Ramsey's phrase. I was driving and penetrating and hitting the open man. My shot found its rhythm. It was like destiny or something. I was the player I knew I could be.

My second biggest problem from outside was overstriding before pulling up for the shot. I'm talking about that last stride before getting off the jump shot. I was so herky-jerky that I was ripping the sides of my sneakers. I shortened my stride. Now I'm not so strung out. It saved a second in the shot. Amazing what that second means.

Now I still go into slumps, but they usually aren't bad. Nothing like 0-for-12. A bad night for me is 5-for-12, say. But I don't shoot much if I'm not on. But when the adrenalin is flowing and my moves are working and I'm feeling I can pop 'em in, I want the ball. I have my streaks and I get psyched up. Like the 1972 season, I went through the early part of the season lackluster. I couldn't hit much. Then I had a stretch of twenty games where I scored 30 or more points. I just had it, even in practice. I'd just look at the basket and it goes in. Guided by radar, man.

Like when I hit 18 for 22 against Buffalo in 1972. People asked me where I was aiming. I say I shoot for the net because that's usually all I hit. Clean through. Unreal. I love it.

There are seven steps to shooting: You catch the ball. You bring it in. You draw it back. You set it out. Your hand is up. You shoot. You follow through.

1. You should get to know your shooting range, how far you can shoot and still be comfortable and reasonably accurate. Never force a shot. Oscar Robertson, for example, rarely shoots from farther than maybe 17 or 18 feet out. That's because he's so strong he can maneuver closer to the basket than most guards. But a Pete Maravich or a Dave DeBusschere have the knack of shooting from 25 or 30 feet, and they can do that without using a dribble to gather momentum. I can shoot from that far too. I developed that from strengthening my wrists and body with weights.

The longest shot I've ever seen in the pros was the one Jerry West made on us in the 1970 playoffs. He heaved a running one-hander from almost full-court in the last second to send the game into overtime. I saw a look in his eyes when he shot it, like he knew it was going in. I said to myself, "Is he crazy?" But it was all correct form. It was a shot, not a throw. The ball swished through. Dave DeBusschere was under the basket and he just crumbled when the ball went in. He actually fell down out of shock. I couldn't move. I just kept staring. I think if West would make that shot all the time, he'd turn the rest of us into zombies. But I think that shot is normally out of shooting range for most of us, including West.

2. Confidence, keeping yourself psyched up, is the thing shooters need. A good shooter never lets a miss or a blocked shot bother him because he figures next time it'll be his turn. But I'm a little different from most. I know when I'm off. So I stop shooting.

Jump-Shot

1. I usually give a slight fake before going up to see what my defensive man is going to do.

2. But when I know I can get my shot off right away, I make my last dribble a hard one to give my body an extra push into the air.

3. I'm balanced, usually with my right foot slightly in front of the left. Knees are bent and I jump up, but without straining. I think I shoot at the top of my jump. But Billy Cunningham shoots on the way down (and so did Elgin Baylor) and Kevin Loughery shoots on the way up. Whatever fits your style.

4 OFFENSIVE PLAYS

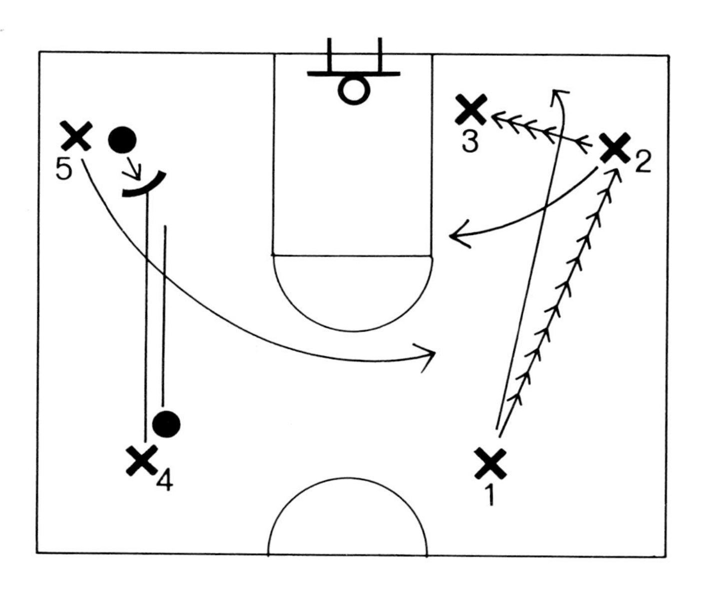

Play using low post. Guard X1 passes to forward X2, who passes to center X3. Then X1 cuts down and X2 cuts off him. Meanwhile X4 runs down and picks forward X5's man. And X5 comes around to give the center three passing options.

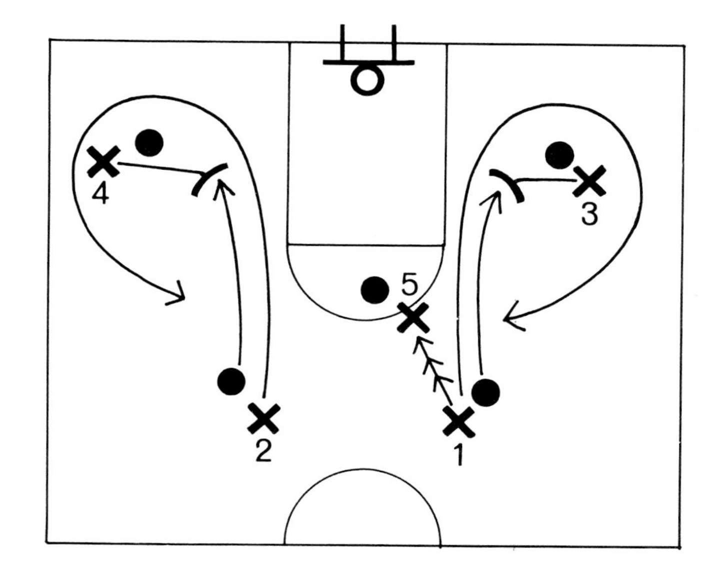

Play using high post. X1 passes to center X5. X3 steps up to pick for X1's defender as X1 runs down, around and back up. X2 and X4 are doing same kind of picking on other side of court.

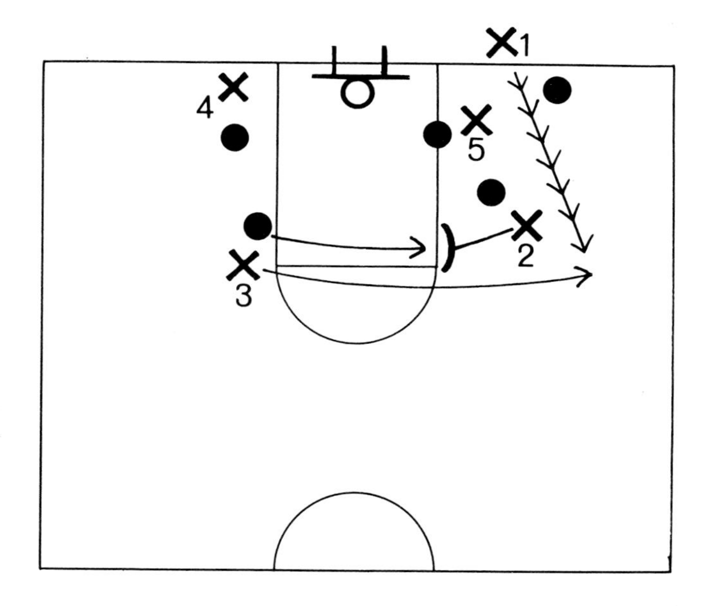

Out-of-bounds play on baseline. X2 picks for X3's man. X2 cuts for ball. X4 and X5 may do the same thing. Or X4 can pick for X5's man.

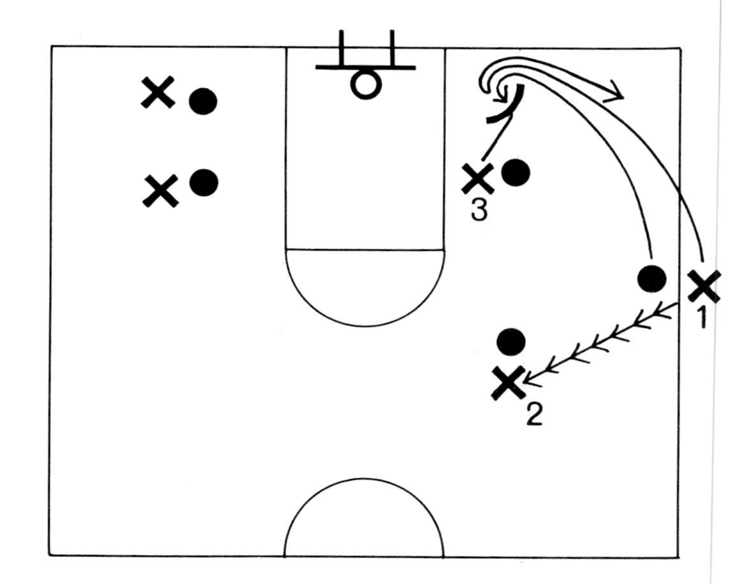

Out-of-bounds play on side. X1 tosses in to X2. X1 then runs down toward center, X3. Then X3 picks X1's man, and X1 comes back to corner to get pass for jump shot X2.

4. Your elbows are comfortably in front of you—not spread out—and you're facing the basket. But sometimes you find the basket on the way up. Like Elvin Hayes, he shoots with his back to the basket and then turns around and there's the basket. The pros have played so long that they usually have a sense of where the basket is. Most of the time I don't think you watch the basket. While you're dribbling you watch the man, and when you go up you find the basket.

5. Some guys aim for the front of the rim. Some shoot for the back. I start out shooting for the back of the rim, usually. Then I get my rhythm and, like I say, it's all net from there. But I never follow the flight of the ball. I think it throws you off. I just watch the basket. All I care about seeing is the ball crackle the net.

6. I shoot with the fingertips and with the fingers spread comfortably.

7. My thumb is just under the ball.

8. I control the ball with my left hand, and keep it there almost to the point of release.

9. Some guys bring the ball way over their head, like Wes Unseld. Some shoot from the back of their head, like Robertson. Some shoot from the hip, like Jerry Lucas, like a shotput. Some guys shoot from behind the ear, like West. I shoot it from about the right side of the top of my head. Wherever you can get if off quickest and easiest.

10. Wrist should be bent back for greater snap.

11. Follow through, bringing the wrist down sharply.

12. You usually shouldn't float. I mean, you normally come down in about the same spot you went up. Sometimes you can't do that, though. Like sometimes you've faked the guy and you're twisting around him while he's in the air and you're double-pumping or something to get a 3-point play.

13. I usually shoot with an arc. First, to get the ball over my defensive man's hands. And second, to give the ball a chance on the rim. If it hits the front of the rim it might bounce, stall and come back in. Cazzie Russell is a great shot, but he shoots bee-liners. He always wants the ball to go straight in. A lot of times he'll get it in and out. It plays back and forth against the rim like it's in a pinball machine. But it depends on the basket. If you've got a tight basket the ball is more likely to go in and out. Milwaukee is like that. But a loose basket is better for a straight-line shooter. Baltimore had loose baskets. And the old Garden, it was like a drop pocket. You shot the ball and it hit the rim and it'd bounce in almost every time.

14. You should have a good spin on the ball. If you use your fingertips you should have a natural backspin. The spin serves the same kind of purpose as the arc. It gives the ball more of a chance to go in. If you shoot a knuckleball it's going to hit and bounce out. Like a knuckleball in baseball is hard to catch. But someone like Frank Selvy shot it flat and it went in. So, like I say, do it your way.

15. I try to hold the ball in the center, or against the seams. You get a better grip that way. It's a matter of feel, and I can get it that way in a split-second. But it's not all that important. It's just one more thing going for you.

16. Sometimes you make up a shot. If I go up to shoot and a guy jumps me, I might put the ball this way or that way and shoot it. Most backcourt men can do that. Most big guys can't. They're in a pattern, they're just one way. They go shoot and that's it. Little guys have to improvise. But then you have the danger of taking bad shots, off-balance shots. But an Oscar Robertson, he shoots the same way every time. And that's why I think he has the best jump-shot I've ever seen. You see, if you have to make up a shot, it's normally a bad shot to start with even if it goes in. You were forcing the shot. The best shot is the one you go straight up for.

Sequence of a jump shot.

The Pearl's head fake.

CHANEY
12

Oscar Robertson: the perfect jump shot.

Driving

You need to be strong. Driving, the first move is explosive. You have to go hard for the basket. Driving isn't easy. I think one of the best drivers is Mike Riordan of the Bullets. He really drives. He goes hard and strong to the basket. You've got to set your man up for the first step, from a standing start.

1. The first step is the most important step in the drive. It gets you past your man if it's done right.

I use what I call the Elgin Baylor move, where you pivot on one foot. Some people call it the rocker step. You show your man the ball to see what his reaction is. As soon as he commits himself—leans any way—you go the other way. Or you can fake a pass or a shot and drive. Fake it and you're gone.

The rocker step is good if you're quicker than the other guy. If not, you could always get the jump-shot, if not the drive. After you get the jump-shot, this is how you get a guy on a string. You shoot once, then fake him, then you drive. So he doesn't know what to expect.

2. Feel your defensive man out. If he's playing with his feet parallel and not staggered, then you know you can usually drive either side of him.

3. The first step should be a big step, longer than normal, to get around the guy.

4. I throw the ball out farther than normal when I start the dribble. Get the ball out in front of you, away from the body.

5. You're allowed to bring your non-dribbling arm up to protect the ball (the ball is of course on the other side of your body away from the defensive man.) That arm is for protection, not to be used as a weapon.

6. The last step and a half might be long or it might be short. It depends on how far you stop dribbling from the baskets. There is no set rule that because the first step is longer the last step should be the same.

7. I make body contact on a drive. After you go around the man you lean into him to slow down his momentum. If you don't you just let him travel behind you, then he maybe can time your jump and maybe block your shot. So I put my body on him.

8. Sometimes you'll drive into a few guys. That's why you have to be under control at all times and take what's there. If the shot's not there, men should be open for a pass. Most of the time I know where everybody is on the court. I'm usually under control. That's my whole game, control.

9. Jumping high for the drive is not usually the most important thing. It's fakery that counts—faking a guy, making him jump off the wrong foot. So to be a good driver, you don't necessarily have to jump that high. Just your moves. Like Barnett is a great driver. He doesn't jump high. If you put your hand here, Dick puts the ball there. He gets it off quick. But Dean Meminger jumps high—even if he's only six-one. But if you can't jump high, then you have to rely on quickness.

10. If I'm bigger than you, I might try to challenge you and jump over you. But some guys, they'll challenge anyone, which is not the policy I recommend. Now, Freddie Carter, he's got a lot of confidence in his jumping ability on the drive. So he'll try to go over Willis or Wilt or anyone. Sometimes he succeeds, but it might be a key moment in a game where he doesn't, like his shot is blocked. I guess it's a matter of pride with those guys. They feel they can just go over somebody.

1 *White moves toward me.*

3 *I stay in original route.*

2 *I throw head and shoulder fake. White stops his progress.*

4 *And continue on.*

What I usually do is go to the side and bank the ball if it's a one-on-one with a bigger guy on me. To me, the safest is the best in that situation. Some other good drivers are West and Clark. Archibald is good for his size. He may go medium-speed into the free-throw line, then he explodes toward the basket and usually makes the shot and draws a foul. He's all speed. Robertson is a good driver, and he's all strength. Connie Hawkins, he's a good driver who uses his jumping ability.

11. Bank the ball off the backboard, usually. It's normally a safer shot. But when guys get bigger, like a lot of pros, they go right up the middle and lay it in the basket, or stuff it in.

12. Going off the wrong foot in the pros is used a lot. Usually, a guy shoots a drive or layup off the opposite foot from the shooting hand. If you shoot righty, you'll be pushing off normally with the left foot. The right foot is the "climbing" foot. Sometimes the pros do it right shot, right-foot push-off. It throws defenders off their rhythm. But you can only do it after you've got the fundamentals down correctly.

13. Improvising is a big thing on drives. Sometimes a guy comes out of nowhere to try to block the shot. So you've got to go into double-pumps and scoops and twists. I don't know how it's done, even though I do them myself. It's instinct.

14. Learn to shoot inside with either hand.

Hook-Shot

I never could shoot a hook-shot.

Moves

Most moves are instinctive. Timing and reflexes. But there are some you can learn the fundamentals of. The 3-point play: I copied a lot of that from Dick Barnett. In his younger days he used to like fake a guy up and as the guy would leave his feet, Dick goes up for the shot. So when I first tried that particular move, I faked the guy up but was never in a position to jump into him. I had the ball too low. The trick is when you fake you should keep the ball high, about shoulder-high, instead of down by the waist. You're facing him. Show him the ball and fake as if you're going to shoot, bringing the ball to your shoulders.

You don't leave your feet until the guy commits himself, until he leans or jumps. Then you jump up and a little bit into him. He's off balance, so there should be contact. Foul on him and you make the basket, then the free throw—3 points.

But be careful that you don't force the play and bang into him when he's on balance. Foul on you. Sometimes I get a little anxious and have an offensive foul called on me.

The guys who are most susceptible to this fake are the great leapers, the guys who like to block shots, like Freddie Carter and John Havlicek. They go in the air a lot on defense. In this instance, their strength becomes their weakness.

Head Fake:

Only a little more exaggerated head nod than on a normal shot. You should look pretty much the same because on this particular move, if I fake the guy and he doesn't jump, then I go up and shoot the ball. So he's really at my mercy. I make the move, he stays down, I go up and make the shot.

Switching hands on the crossover dribble: It's very seldom used today because most guys use the behind-the-back or the spin. On this particular move you have to use the head-and-shoulder fakes as well as the feet. It's like running in place. You come down and shake. You lean hard one way, then push off the forward foot and you switch the ball to the other hand. And you go.

It's a dangerous play because you have the ball out in front of you. You've got to be a good dribbler to do it. Archie Clark does it the best. And he's about the only one who does it regularly. But it's a sucker move. It's you or him. So you've got to have confidence in yourself that you can beat the guy.

I come cutting close off a pick from Jerry Lucas, as Jerry West pursues.

Spin

Monroe started the spinner. In the old days it was a cardinal sin. The coach said that if you put your back to your man another defensive man could leap in and take the ball away. But now the guys are so good on offense, you can pretty much tell where the defense is. So if you've got your back to a guy and think the side is clear, it should be clear.

We clear the side when The Pearl is going into orbit. I normally do it when a guy is crowding me or overplaying me to my left or right, then I'll spin around him. You have to react to his reaction. If he's not exactly behind me, I might fake right and go left, or fake left and go right.

In the Pivot

When a small man switches on me, I usually give him a fake and bank the ball in off the backboard.

I don't mind when a big guy is on me either when I happen to go into the pivot. I feel I can beat him with quickness. I fake sharp and distinct. But if he doesn't go for my fakes and if I don't have a shot, I get the ball out of there. That's what I often do when I have Dave Cowens in the pivot. He's quick, so I get the ball out of there.

Stutter Move

That's when you give some quick hard dribbles and for a second you're not going anywhere but waiting for your man to commit himself. It's a good move and I use it a lot on fast-breaks and semi-breaks. It leads to one of my best shots.

A lot of times I'll have the guy falling back and I take the jumper. I'll do this on a three-on-two fast-break, for instance, because we have two guys coming from the sides to crash the boards in case of a miss.

Dunk Shots

I have nothing against dunk shots. Only danger is like if you're in a crowd and you try to go in and try to dunk against a Chamberlain, you've lost a shot. You run the risk of getting hurt because in a dunk you've got a lot of momentum going to the basket and if a guy blocks it there's a possibility that you may be slammed straight to the floor. So I guess when you're all alone it's all right to dunk. Sometimes even that doesn't pay. Wilt once stole a ball and went the length of the court and I guess he got tired from dribbling—he's not used to that—and he went up for a dunk, hit the ball on the bottom of the rim and fell to the floor. He still held the ball. Not only did he miss the dunk, he was called for traveling.

Another time I saw a guy break his finger trying to dunk. So I just try to lay the ball up nice and easy. Too many risks involved to get an *ooh* from the crowd for dunking. To me, the safer the cooler.

Foul Shots

Free throws are strange. Wilt, for one, even talked to a psychiatrist about his foul-shooting problems. Sometimes I can be at the line and I know that I'm feeling fine and I shoot it up and it's all bottoms. Clean in. Another time I'm on the line and my shirt strap doesn't feel right and my pants all of a sudden feel tight and my feet can't get comfortable and it feels like I'm standing in mud. You're standing there and the pace of the game has slowed and all there is is quiet and pressure.

Normally I don't practice free throws very much. I think free throws are within you. You don't need to practice fifty or a hundred free throws every day. Free-throw shooting all depends on the pressure, whether or not you press in tight situations. I think the main thing is confidence in free throws. It's not enough to tell yourself you're going to make it when you step to the line. You got to believe it.

Different guys have different techniques. Hal Greer takes a jump-shot for a free throw. Dick Barnett like curtsies before shooting. Henry Bibby shoots from the right side of the line. Wilt stands nearly at the top of the key. Rick Barry shoots

Bill Bradley concentrates at foul line.

underhanded. But most guys are like me. They shoot one-handed. I follow a set routine: I'm just thinking of getting in the right frame of mind for a free throw. I go up there casually, loose. I watch the scoreboard and see what's going on in a given situation. I give myself a quick briefing of the game—the score, how much time is left, the times out left.

I get the feel of the ball. I bounce it a few times, maybe take a deep breath to relax. Inhale or exhale. It depends. Maybe sometimes in the beginning of the game I'm not winded, so there's no need to take a deep breath. I bend my knees. I watch the back of the rim. I shoot. I roll the ball off my fingertips with perfect control and get a nice backspin and soft arc. All rhythm, all one motion.

In practice I'll maybe take five or ten free throws, unless I'm in a slump. Then I'll shoot more. But even jump-shots I don't shoot much in practice. And when things are going well in games I practice shooting hardly at all. That's because I get bored of shooting. I'm not one that can go out and just shoot, shoot, shoot. My arm gets tired and my patience isn't good. I think that's one reason why I sometimes get slumps in free throws, lack of concentration. In free throws you have to concentrate really more than jump-shots. In jump-shots it's mostly instinct because there's a guy all over you and you just shoot. Whereas in free throws you're just there, like starting a show all by yourself, you got time to think. A lot of times it's a problem because you overdo it. It's not walking the ball and dribbling it and shooting it, bang.

But like in the 1972 season. I shot 80 percent from the free-throw line during the season. But in the playoffs I hit a slump and dropped to 50 percent. I can't explain it. Maybe I was concentrating too much.

So I try not to take too much time on the free-throw line. I don't want to think too much and have the basket start blurring. You can think yourself out of a shot.

Fast-Break

The only way to run the fast-break most of the time is to keep the ball in the center of the floor, with the middleman. I take the ball straight down the middle. The other guys' jobs are to fill the lanes. There are three lanes to consider. So you have one guy running on one side of the floor, another guy running on the other side and me in the middle. I try to get the middle position because I'm the team's ballhandler. But if I can't get there, then someone else has to take it and I become a wingman or a trailer.

You can't run a fast-break with the ball on the side of the court. You cut off one of your alternatives and make it easier for the defense. So the ball should always be in the middle of the court with the middleman.

Now, when the man with the ball comes to the free-throw line he can pass to either side or he can stop and take a jump shot or he can keep driving for the basket. Well, you take whatever the defense gives you.

Like if it's a three-on-one or three-on-two and if you're the top man on defense I shouldn't try to challenge you. If I stand there I should pass the ball to the wingman. So now you have to react to that move. You've got to do something. If you stay on me, the other opposite wingman should go straight to the basket for the layup because the backman on defense has to go out and get the guy with the ball. And if he doesn't come out we have an easy jump-shot anyway. But it's the defense's job to give us anything but a layup.

I like to give up the ball because then your guys will run down harder to fill the lanes when they know they might get a shot. Also, it puts more pressure on the defensive guys. Whereas if I try to jive around and challenge you with a drive or start spinning, I might lose the ball or lose my fast-break advantage since you'll have your guys hurrying back on defense.

The break often begins after one team has missed a shot. The first most important thing is the outlet pass. The rebounder has to whip the

Willis Reed relaxes at the foul line.

Start of fast break. I take the ball into the middle lane.

ball out to a teammate. Wes Unseld is about the best in the NBA with the outlet pass. He can throw a fast two-handed push-pass or a baseball pass to get things going. But the fast-break has to be controlled. You see some teams throwing the ball wildly all over the place. It's like a dodge 'em game.

But I like a two-on-one break where there's no dribbling. Just passing short between teammates. And the defensive guy is put into a revolving door. Where as a lot of guys like to dribble until the last minute.

MISCELLANEOUS OFFENSE

JUMP BALL

When jumping, it's all timing. As soon as the referee lets the ball go, you go off. You've got to be alert. Some guys try to hold you down, hold onto your body or step on your toes. It could mess up your jump. But the ref will usually call that. So the tricks don't pay.

When on the outside, be aware that some jumpers tip off where they're going to tap a ball. I watch the other team's jumper and if I think I can get it, or if I know my man can get it, then I get in position and keep my man behind me. But if I think he can't get it, I look at the guy that's tipping the ball. A lot of times you see in his eyes where the ball's going.

Or when he looks around to see who's there you can see his eyes set on one spot. I can pretty well figure that he's going to tap the ball there. So when the ball goes up, I'll just move in that spot. Especially in an obvious mismatch, like Hawkins against Bradley, you know who's going to get the tip, Connie. So you adjust.

Playing Offense Without the Ball

A lot of guys don't know how to do this, and they're useless without the ball. There are a lot of stars but very few can play without the ball. They don't know how to position for rebound or where to go to balance the court on defense or what to do when a guy is face-guarding you.

It's very seldom that a guy can pressure me and force me out of my game to play herky-jerky or helter-skelter. Only for maybe a minute or so before I regroup. So there are very few times when I've been really flustered on offense from a guy playing good defense. Usually a guy like Joe Caldwell, when he was in the league, would try to face-guard me all the time. He was so close I could practically feel his breath. So what I did was go without the ball and run for maybe five or ten minutes until he got tired, then I'd start going for the ball. You know, like he's wasted a lot of energy because there's pressure on him to follow me. Some teams felt that since I handled the ball 80 percent of the time, the way to beat the Knicks was to keep Clyde from the ball.

So I wouldn't struggle to get the ball necessarily. I'd let Barnett or Monroe take it down. I'd just go and run regular plays and later in the game this guy was tired because of concentrating so hard, whereas I was rested. Bradley is very good at moving without the ball. We also rely on picks to spring a man loose from a close defender.

Sometimes I'll tell Bradley I think I can beat the defensive man back-door, so we set him up for that.

When a guy face-guards you he is always vulnerable for the back-door because he doesn't see the ball: he's only watching you. Fake like you're going toward the ball. Take a step away from the hoop and make him react and then just go straight to the hoop. You don't pivot, but run straight forward.

Shooting Practice

I like to try different things because I get bored very easily when I'm shooting alone. When I work out I incorporate dribbling, moves and shooting in one.

I'll dribble it down the middle, maybe give a head-fake then pull up at the top of the key, shoot. Other guys might move around in a circle, like one spot here, one spot there. I envision an imaginary man guarding me and I'm bringing the ball up. I'm moving, not standing. I drive for the basket. And I'm not dribbling in front of me, I'm protecting the ball. I'm keeping the ball away from the imaginary man. But I don't practice shooting that much. My arm gets tired. So I shoot some lefty. Otherwise I feel lopsided.

Off on Shooting

I remember the beginning of the 1971–72 season I kept coming up short on shots. I missed a lot of easy shots by hitting the front rim. I think I wasn't in the best condition, my legs weren't responding like they should have. My legs felt heavy, real heavy. I didn't run enough in the off-season. I waited until the last two weeks of August to get in shape. So the next summer it was different. I ran almost every day.

And I started off the season great. First game I made six steals, took seven rebounds, made seven assists and hit on 8 out of 13 from the field. I was flyin'. My whole thing is being in shape. Then the rest of my stuff will come.

In practice, when I'm slumping, I try to go back to the fundamentals. Like once I went into a slump, I kind of lost my rhythm, and then some of my confidence. I saw game films and compared them to when I was hitting. I saw I had become lazy unconsciously and wasn't jumping as high as I normally did on my jump-shot. That threw my shot off just a bit, but enough.

Every shot I miss I immediately run through my mind. Why? Off balance? Too far away? Like once Connie Hawkins came out of nowhere just when I was releasing the ball. I jerked the shot, and missed. I said to Connie, "Hey, man, don't scare me like that."

Loose Balls

Just hustle. Don't try to dribble before you get it under control. Like if a loose ball is rolling around the floor, you should pick it up and then dribble. Most guys will start dribbling it before they get control.

Setting a screen

YORK
10

Out-of-Bounds

When a ball is going out-of-bounds, a lot of guys will always try to throw the ball back even if they don't have a teammate clear.

If I steal or retrieve a ball and my momentum is taking me out-of-bounds and if I don't have a specific man to throw to, I won't throw it back when I'm on defense, but I will throw it back if I'm on offense.

On defense you might throw it to the other team and that creates a five-on-four situation that they might be able to take quick advantage of. But when we're on offense, even if I throw it to the other team, all of us (including me) still have plenty of time to get back on defense. The other team will get the ball even if I don't throw it back, so it's a safe gamble.

Out-of-Bounds Baseline Throw-In

When you throw the ball from out-of-bounds, don't stand under the backboard. An intended long pass by you could end up hitting you on the head.

Statistics

WALT FRAZIER

Born March 29, 1945. Height 6:04. Weight 205.
Alma Mater—Southern Illinois '67.
Drafted by New York on first round, 1967.

REGULAR SEASON

Sea.	Team	G	MIN	FGA	FGM	PCT	FTA	FTM	PCT	REB	A	PF	DISQ	PTS	AVG
67-69	New York	74	1588	568	256	.451	235	154	.655	313	305	199	2	666	9.0
68-69	New York	80	2949	1052	531	.505	457	341	.756	499	535	245	2	1403	17.5
69-70	New York	77	3040	1158	600	.518	547	409	.748	465	629	203	1	1609	20.9
70-71	New York	80	3455	1317	651	.494	557	434	.779	544	536	240	1	1736	21.7
71-72	New York	77	3126	1307	669	:512	557	450	.808	513	446	185	0	1788	23.2
72-73	New York	78	3181	1389	681	.490	350	286	.817	570	461	186	0	1648	21.1
Totals		466	17339	6791	3388	.499	2703	2074	.767	2904	3012	1258	6	8850	19.0

PLAYOFF RECORD

Sea.	Team	G	MIN	FGA	FGM	PCT	FTA	FTM	PCT	REB	A	PF	DISQ	PTS	AVG
67-68	New York	4	119	33	12	.364	18	14	.778	22	25	12	0	38	9.5
68-69	New York	10	415	177	89	.503	57	34	.596	74	91	30	0	212	21.2
69-70	New York	19	834	247	118	.478	89	68	.764	139	146	42	0	304	16.0
70-71	New York	12	501	204	108	.529	75	55	.733	70	54	45	0	271	22.6
71-72	New York	16	704	276	148	.536	125	92	.736	112	98	48	0	388	24.3
72-73	New York	17	765	292	150	.514	94	73	.777	124	106	52	1	373	21.9
Totals		78	3338	1229	625	.509	458	336	.734	551	530	240	1	1586	20.3

ALL-STAR GAME RECORD

Sea.	Team	G	MIN	FGA	FGM	PCT	FTA	FTM	PCT	REB	A	PF	DISQ	PTS	AVG
1970	New York		24	7	3	.700	2	1	.500	3	4	2	0	7	
1971	New York		26	9	3	.333	0	0	.000	6	5	2	0	6	
1972	New York		25	11	7	.636	2	1	.500	3	5	2	0	15	
1973	New York		26	15	5	.333	0	0	.000	6	1	1	0	10	
Totals			101	32	18	.429	4	2	.500	18	15	7	0	38	

MATCHING UP THE FOUR BEST

It is commonly believed that Frazier, Robertson, West and Cousy are the four finest guards to play in "the modern era," which usually is considered from the advent of the 24-second clock in October, 1954.

Following is a comparison of their pro records in regular season and playoff games:

REGULAR SEASON

	Yrs. Played	G	MIN	FGA	FGM	PCT	FTA	FTM	PCT	REB	AST	PF	DISQ	PTS	AVG
Walter Frazier	6	466	17339	3388	6791	.499	2074	2703	.767	2904	3012	1258	6	8850	19.0
Oscar Robertson	13	970	41392	9170	18848	.487	7482	8931	.838	7525	9441	2799	18	25822	26.6
Jerry West	13	902	35605	8784	18513	.474	6995	8603	.813	5250	6032	2355	17	24563	27.2
*Bob Cousy	13	924	30264	16468	6168	.375	5756	4624	.803	4794	6959	2242	20	16960	18.4

PLAYOFFS

	G	MIN	FGA	FGM	PCT	FTA	FTM	PCT	REB	AST	PF	DISQ	PTS	AVG
Walter Frazier	78	3338	625	1229	.509	336	458	.734	551	530	240	1	1586	20.3
Oscar Robertson	70	2984	585	1226	.462	516	603	.856	524	620	221	3	1686	24.1
Jerry West	152	6307	1620	3451	.469	1213	1507	.805	853	969	450	3	4453	29.3
*Bob Cousy	109	3940	2116	689	.326	799	640	.801	546	937	314	4	2018	18.5

*The only retired player as of this writing (1973).

FRAZIER HONORS

LITTLE ALL-AMERICA, FIRST TEAM, '66-'67
(AP and UPI)

LITTLE ALL-AMERICA, SECOND TEAM, '64-'65
(Associated Press)

ALL ROOKIE TEAM 1967-68

(with Earl Monroe — Baltimore
Phil Jackson — Knicks
Bob Ruhl — Seattle
Al Tucker — Seattle)

NIT MOST VALUABLE PLAYER, 1967

ALL NBA DEFENSIVE TEAM
First Team Five Straight Years

ALL-NBA
First Team 69-70. 71-72

MY 4 FAVORITE PRO GAMES

NATIONAL BASKETBALL ASSOCIATION
OFFICIAL SCORER'S REPORT
APRIL 22, 1973

KNICKS (117)

	min	fgm	fga	ftm	fta	reb	a	pf	pts
Barnett	4	1	2	0	0	0	0	1	2
Bibby	14	1	3	0	0	0	0	1	2
Bradley	33	5	17	3	3	4	3	5	13
Frazier	57	15	30	7	12	9	4	5	37
Gianelli	16	4	4	2	4	3	1	1	10
Jackson	20	3	4	2	4	4	0	1	8
DeBuschr	51	8	17	6	6	10	3	3	22
Lucas	15	0	2	3	4	3	1	1	3
Meminger	38	4	7	2	5	5	7	6	10
Reed	42	5	11	0	0	9	2	6	10
Total	290	46	97	25	38	47	21	30	117

BOSTON (110)

	min	fgm	fga	ftm	fta	reb	a	pf	pts
Chaney	30	2	6	0	0	3	5	6	4
Cowens	55	14	29	5	7	14	2	6	33
Finkel	3	0	0	0	0	1	0	0	0
Kuberski	25	3	7	0	0	2	0	3	6
Nelson	53	6	14	4	4	5	2	5	16
Silas	49	2	9	1	2	23	5	2	5
Westphal	19	3	7	0	0	1	1	4	6
White	46	12	31	10	10	7	6	6	34
Williams	10	3	4	0	0	3	2	3	6
Total	290	45	107	20	23	59	23	35	110

Boston	20	28	24	17	12	9—110
Knicks	25	17	14	33	12	16—117

Referees—Jack Madden and Jake O'Donnell.

Sunday, April 22, 1973. We win in double overtime to take 3-1 lead in division final playoffs. We were down 76-60 with 10 minutes left in the last quarter. I scored 15 points in the last quarter. We tied the game. And I got 10 more points in the overtime.

NATIONAL BASKETBALL ASSOCIATION
OFFICIAL SCORER'S REPORT
NOVEMBER 9, 1972

KNICKS (101)

	min	fgm	fga	ftm	fta	reb	a	pf	pts
Bibby	8	0	2	0	0	1	1	1	0
Bradley	41	8	20	1	1	5	3	2	17
DeBschre	43	8	21	2	3	10	4	4	18
Frazier	40	13	24	9	10	11	9	3	35
Gianelli	2	0	1	0	0	1	0	0	0
Jackson	8	2	6	0	0	6	1	0	4
Lucas	33	6	13	0	0	8	3	3	12
Meminger	10	1	2	0	0	2	1	1	2
Monroe	38	6	15	1	2	4	5	3	13
Reed	17	0	5	0	0	5	0	3	9
Total	240	44	109	13	16	53	27	20	101

ATLANTA (99)

	min	fgm	fga	ftm	fta	reb	a	pf	pts
Bellamy	24	1	5	0	0	6	0	2	2
Bracey	9	4	6	0	0	1	0	1	8
Christian	24	4	5	1	1	11	0	4	9
Gilliam	32	9	15	2	2	8	4	2	20
Hudson	39	8	22	7	7	5	3	1	23
Maravich	42	10	23	5	7	8	4	4	25
Mast	7	0	1	0	0	2	2	0	0
Trapp	26	2	11	3	5	4	4	4	7
Washgton	37	2	10	1	1	15	0	0	5
Total	240	40	98	19	23	60	17	18	99

Atlanta	27	30	15	27— 99
Knicks	21	17	30	33—101

Referees—Richie Powers and Alan Brunkhorst.

We were trailing by nearly 20 points at halftime. I scored 27 of my 35 points in the second half. I was stealing balls, hitting the open man. And against the team from my home town.

NATIONAL BASKETBALL ASSOCIATION
OFFICIAL SCORER'S REPORT
FEBRUARY 10, 1968

KNICKS (115)

	min	fgm	fga	ftm	fta	reb	a	pf	pts
Barnett (G)	38	7	15	5	8	3	3	4	19
Bellamy (C)	44	9	18	6	7	21	4	3	24
Bradley	6	1	5	0	0	0	0	2	2
Frazier (G)	39	9	18	5	5	15	15	3	23
Jackson, P.	13	3	3	0	2	3	0	2	6
Komives	13	1	4	2	2	1	2	2	4
Reed (F)	39	6	10	3	4	12	0	3	15
Russell (F)	15	6	7	1	3	3	4	3	13
Van Arsdale	33	4	8	1	2	3	2	4	9
Total	240	46	88	23	33	65	30	26	115

PHILADELPHIA (97)

	min	fgm	fga	ftm	fta	reb	a	pf	pts
Chamberlain (C)	46	8	18	0	3	12	7	2	16
Cunningham	33	4	17	4	6	17	1	4	12
Green	15	3	6	1	2	2	1	0	7
Greer (G)	41	6	18	3	6	2	5	5	15
Guokas (G)	39	4	6	2	3	5	1	3	10
Jackson, L. (F)	21	2	7	0	0	8	3	6	4
Melchionni	16	3	6	2	2	0	3	2	8
Walker (F)	29	10	18	5	7	8	2	1	25
Total	240	40	96	17	29	55	23	23	97

Knicks	34	19	29	32—115
Philadelphia	20	23	23	31— 97

Referees—Norm Drucker and Manny Sokol

The seventh and deciding game of the 1969-70 NBA championship playoff.

NATIONAL BASKETBALL ASSOCIATION
OFFICIAL SCORER'S REPORT
MAY 4, 1970

KNICKS (107)

	min	fgm	fga	ftm	fta	reb	a	pf	pts
Barnett (G)	44	6	17	4	5	0	3	3	16
Bowman	7	0	2	1	1	4	0	2	1
Bradley (F)	38	7	15	9	3	7	2	4	16
DeBusschere (F)	36	6	21	0	0	6	2	5	12
Frazier (G)	46	9	14	3	3	7	12	3	21
Hosket	4	0	2	0	0	0	0	0	0
Reed (C)	8	2	5	3	3	0	1	0	7
Riordan	15	1	1	0	0	0	0	0	2
Russell	32	8	14	4	4	8	5	4	20
Stallworth	19	6	12	0	0	6	3	3	12
Warren	8	0	0	0	0	0	0	1	0
Total	240	45	103	17	19	38	28	25	107

LOS ANGELES (100)

	min	fgm	fga	ftm	fta	reb	a	pf	pts
Baylor (F)	43	8	15	5	6	11	5	2	21
Chamberlain (C)	45	9	12	4	9	19	3	2	22
Counts	12	0	4	1	1	4	0	2	1
Egan	13	2	2	2	2	0	3	3	6
Erickson (F)	40	3	6	1	2	4	6	4	7
Garrett (G)	33	7	12	4	4	5	0	4	18
Tresvant	8	0	1	5	7	0	0	2	5
West (G)	46	6	14	8	9	2	4	2	20
Total	240	35	66	30	40	45	21	21	100

Knicks	20	20	35	32—107
Los Angeles	30	23	29	18—100

Referees—Mendy Rudolph and Richie Powers

Last game at the old Madison Square Garden on 50th St. This was the first game that I put all the elements of my play together, and I proved to myself that I could be a well-rounded pro.

Rockin' Steady: Game Day

When you're playing good, you can't sleep too long because you can't wait to wake up. You're excited. You can't wait for the next game, the next day. It's really funny, when you're going good you don't mind those games coming up. But when you're in a slump and things drag, it seems they've scheduled three games in one day. That's when even ten hours sleep isn't enough. You want to stay in the rack for twenty-four hours. But that's very seldom. Usually I can't wait to get my act going again.

I'll wake up at about eleven or eleven-thirty to a rock album—unless I've been out last night with soothing music or no music and my head can't stand the rock. Then I'll play jazz. Then I'll take a shower to get me going some more. Make a couple phone calls. Check out the weather and decide to wear something to fit my mood. Sometimes it takes me an hour to sort through my closet to select the right ensemble.

I may run a few errands, maybe pick up a package or send one from the post office across the street. Then I might go down and dust off my Rolls-Royce; it's the last one they made of this model, the 1965 Silver Cloud III. It's all English body and it has four speeds. Not like some of the later-model Rollses that resemble American cars with push-button windows and stuff like that. It cost heavy numbers, $20,000. But it's supposed to last a lifetime. Or if I want to sell it I should be able to get more than what I paid for it. So it's really a bargain. Red leather seats. A dashboard like an instrument panel. A hard-cover instruction manual. I've got two adjoining parking spaces in the lot under my apartment building. That's for extra precaution against nicks. What sold me on the Rolls was the color, burgundy on the lower part, antelope on the upper.

I've got a driver, Tony, who handles bookings for All-Star Sports. I call Tony when I don't want to drive the car myself. But I enjoy driving it. I might be the only guy who drives around Manhattan for pleasure. I roll up the windows and slip in my tape deck and I don't hear the blare and crash of the city. The ride is smooth, like rolling along on a magic carpet. It's always a beautiful day inside that car.

It's nothing like the first car I ever owned. That was in 1962, when I was a senior in high school. A friend and I saved up a hundred bucks each and went partners in a 1949 two-door blue Ford Coupe. It wasn't a bad-looking car, and it had a jazzy long stick shift. The only problem with it was it wouldn't run. I was the one who suffered most because my friend didn't drive. So when the car broke down I was usually the guy responsible.

I had always wanted a hot rod, that was the cool thing in school. We were going to buy big tires and jack up the end. But the tires were too expensive, and if we jacked the car up any higher it would have become an airplane, that's how disjointed it was. There was another reason we didn't jack it up. We couldn't afford a jack. Or even a spare tire.

But I still thought the car looked nice. And I even thought it impressed some girls. Until they rode in it. Then it broke down or it wouldn't start. It was embarrassing. I had the car a year, but it was only on the road about three months. The rest of the time it was in the repair shop.

I used to have to park it on top of a hill so that I'd be sure it would start with a push.

My eldest sister, Mary, remembers one time when she was late and asked me to carry her someplace. I told her I would if she'd push my car to get it started. She pushed and the car started, but I never came back around the corner to get her. I admit it. But there was a reason. She and my other sisters were always on my case about that car. They said it was beneath them to ride in it. So the one time one of them needed a ride, that was the time I was able to get back at them.

I learned a lesson from that old Ford: Never buy a raggedy car. That's why I enjoy my Rolls so much. Although the first time I brought my new Rolls to training camp the battery went dead. And I didn't know where the battery was. I finally had to call the Rolls man. He told me the battery was in the trunk. This was embarrassing too. Some of my teammates and some other admirers of the car were watching and laughing. Clyde Frazier, Mr. Cool. It was like being behind the wheel of that '49 Ford again. But the Rolls hasn't quit on me since.

When I wheel the Rolls into a gas station I'll sometimes order "petrol." That shakes up the attendant. The car takes special oil, and they say that if you go on a long trip you'd better bring along special gear. I heard that a guy and his Rolls were stranded in the country once and he needed a two-dollar water hose and they charged him $100 for it. He had no choice. He paid.

Once I was washing the car down and I was decked out in a yellow cap and clogs. A guy comes over who dug the car and begins asking questions about it. It turns out he thought I was the chauffeur. That's all right. Another time I'm driving this girl in the car and I have to run out

Top: My first car would only start with an effort. Below: Times have changed. I even have a special license plate now. All it says is: WCF.

and get something in a store. She told me when I got back that a kid came up to her and he said seriously, "I've seen rich people before, lady, but no one like you who can afford Clyde Frazier for a chauffeur!"

I'll take the car for a little spin through the park. I don't mind the city streets. I'm in no hurry. I just let all the cars blow by. I'll stop maybe at the Stitching Horse where I might have a pair of antelope pants being made. Or at the Comfort suede-leather store on East 61st Street where I may go for a fitting for a lambskin suit. Or I'll pick up some kicks at the Blacksmith.

Every once in a while I'll think about the game. Who the guards are that I'm going up against. What I'll be doing. I try to keep it loose, don't want to get uptight.

I come back to the apartment and park my wheels. It's about two-thirty. Then I hoof it over to P. J. Clark's or The King of the Sea, if I want seafood, or P. J. O'Hara's or Duncan's (that's Tucker Frederickson's place) for a good steak. Then back to the apartment. I put on some soft rock. I take a hot bath for two minutes. Any more and it'll sap me of energy. But two minutes is enough to relax me so that I can nap. And especially at the beginning of the season it's soothing for the back and the legs if they're sore. Then I lie down and meditate and relax with the music. I sleep for about an hour. I use an alarm clock and I usually take the phone off the hook. I used to get so nervous before games I'd stare at the ceiling all during my nap. But the older I get the more relaxed I am before games. Sometimes now I'll be listening to the music and I can't sleep. So I turn the music off. As soon as the alarm rings I bang the music on again. Usually it's rock again. But sometimes I get so much of rock I get a headache.

It's a way of life getting pepped up for the game. Now, jazz to me is soothing, it doesn't pep me up. Before I leave for the game I put on jazz because I don't want to get too psyched up too soon. I don't want to leave my game in the apartment. So in the morning or afternoon rock is all right. I can reach a peak but then I come back down and it builds up again at the game.

So it's about four-thirty or five now. I pick what I'm going to wear to the game. What's my mood? If I feel like steppin' out I'll wear something gay, maybe a Clyde-type ensemble. Maybe I'll do seals or minks, doing it all when I'm feeling good. But when I haven't been playing good, nothing else interests me. Not dressing up, not chicks—nothing means nothing. If it's raining I may even wear a pair of Puma Clydes to the game. One night it was pouring down like the world was about to end. So I showed up for the game in an old raggedy trenchcoat and sneakers. Usually, I show up dazzling. So now Willis gives me this funny stare. He asked me if this was the new Clyde look.

The sneakers I wore to the game weren't the same ones I wore *in* the game. I usually pick out a snappy color for the game. But lately I've been in to the orange with blue stripe—the Knick colors—for home games.

So now my mind is just wandering as I go through my closet and get my playing gear. I'm sort of thinking about things in general, trying not to think about the game. Only during the playoffs are you concentrating on your man. Playoffs are different, and you know it's only a few games. So then you think about a guy a lot. You see, you're going to play him four straight at least.

I'm ready to leave a little before six. That will give me plenty of time. My thing is, I never like to rush. Always leave myself enough time so if something happens, I have enough time to still be at the game. We have to be dressed by seven. Some guys, at ten to seven they'll be running in. They dress and they're on the floor. Bam. Before you can relax it's game time. I don't like to do that.

I hop the subway train. I don't take my Rolls or a cab to the Garden. Too much of a hassle. It's forty-five minutes if I try to drive through the traffic from my apartment. And once I get to the Garden the kids will be touching and grabbing at

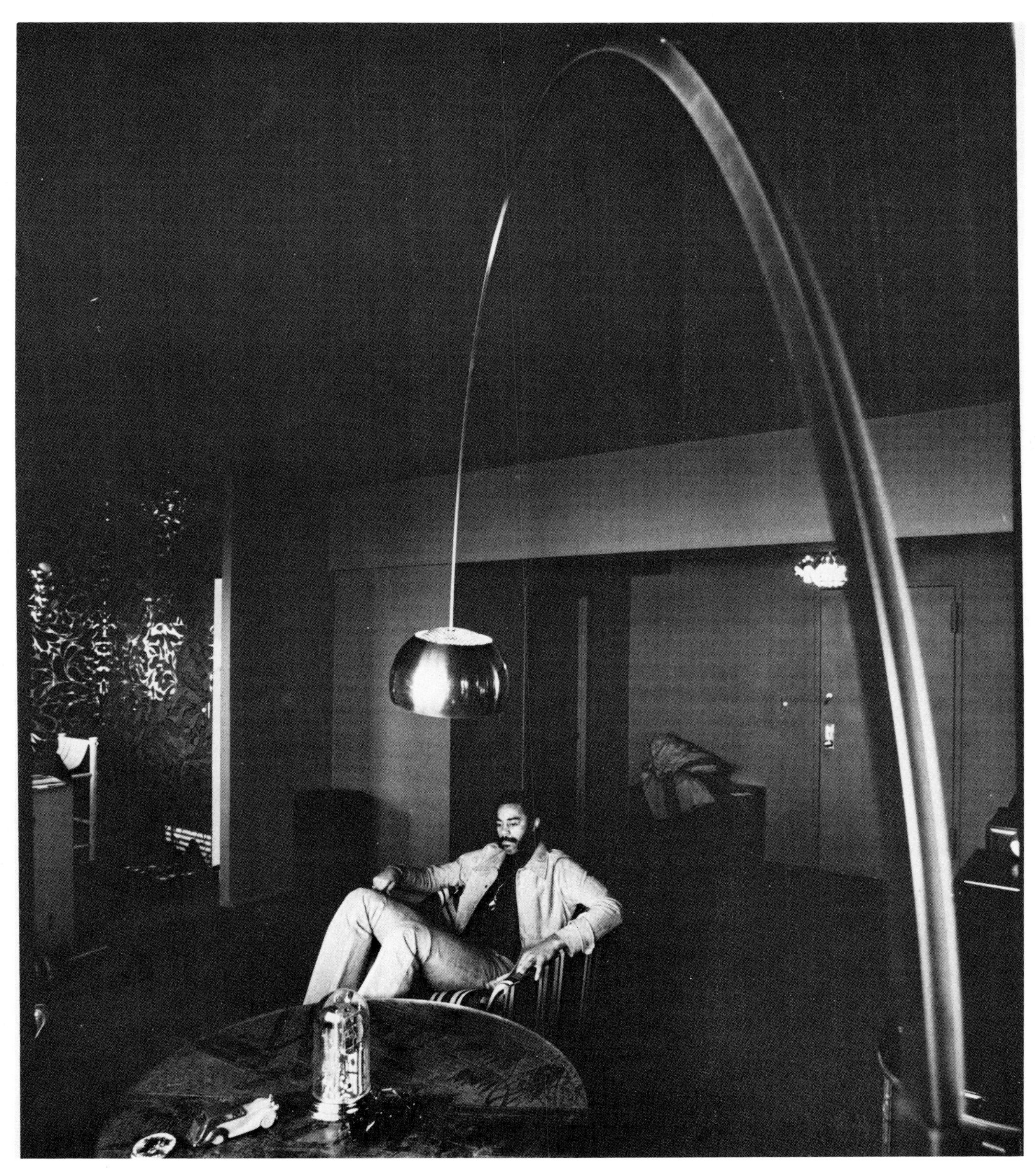

My living room. I like to keep it dark like a night club.

Quick energy from the candy jar.

the car. How would a Rolls look with fingerprints on the window?

The subway takes about fifteen minutes and I can leave my place later than if I went by car or cab. I also save seven dollars a night in parking fees. I live a block from the 53rd Street subway station and the "E" train drops me right at the Garden. I like to walk to the station because it loosens me up, and I get psyched up. The storekeepers and the people on the street are saying things to me. Like a guy will say, "I want 30 points tonight." Or, "Clyde, crunch 'em tonight or I'll crunch you." I get threats like that. Then there's the guy who owns the seafood restaurant and he comes out and says, "Clyde, beat 'em tonight and I'll give you an extra shrimp in your cocktail." See, I get bribes, too. It psyches me up. I couldn't get that by driving to the game in a car. And I rarely have anyone hassle me on the subway. People look and then figure it's not me. They can't believe Clyde Frazier's riding the subway, even when I'm wearing my mink.

A lot of times I'm excited about seeing the game film. It's not mandatory to watch it, but it's on in the locker room right on the wall while the guys are dressing in the light. Film starts at six-thirty. It shows the last time we played this particular team. So if I had a good game and I thought I made good moves, I'll come in early to tape my ankles so I can watch the whole show. Or if I had a bad move, I want to watch to see how the guy beat me. There are certain pointers you can pick up. If you've had a real bad game you don't want to watch that. Too depressing. But if I've had a few bad games, Red will call me in and say, "Let's sit down and watch the film together."

I may go through some of my mail. Once I got 98 letters in a day. I get mail from all over. Some terrific letters. Mostly from kids, and most want a picture or an autograph. I send what they want, although sending my uniform, as one kid in Ohio asked for, is tough. Sometimes they want the request filled in haste. Like one kid in California said, "Please send a picture of the hold Knicks fast. I will be wayting for them."

And sometimes they'll make little mistakes. Like this letter:

Dear Walt Frazier:
I am 6 years old. You are my best player in hockey. Will you please give me your autogph picture.
Your pal. Mike.

Meanwhile guys are coming in and starting to get dressed. The first game of the 1972 season, Julius Erving came into town late, so I tried to get him a ticket. Bill Bradley had a spare and asked if anyone wanted it. I told him I'd give him an extra shot if he let me have the ticket. He handed it over. Then I told the ballboy to take the ticket upstairs and that I'd tip him later. He knows I'm good for it. But our publicity man, Jimmy Wergeles, needled me, "Is it true, Clyde, that you spend all your money in the bank?" I didn't dignify that with an answer.

The talk in the locker room will usually go something like this:

Our trainer, Danny Whelan, calls over to Lucas that he had stayed up late to watch Luke on a late-night television show. Lucas didn't stay up because he had taped it that afternoon.

"Disgusting, what happened?" said Whelan.

"Yeah," said Lucas. He had come on at the end of the show. "I got two minutes of air time. In between 32 commercials. They had promised me 14 minutes. I couldn't do my stuff in two minutes. And I didn't want to talk."

Lucas has some phenomenal tricks. One is memorizing the Manhattan telephone book (he's about half-way through it). Another trick is taking a word and immediately pronouncing it alphabetically. "Basketball" is "aabbekllss."

"I would never go on that show," said Whelan. "The nerve. You should've gone around the corner to that other show. I would've."

Dave DeBusschere comes in.

"I fell asleep, Luke, how'd you do last night?"

"I did the Casper the Ghost act."

"Benched?" asked DeBusschere.
"Almost. Got two minutes." Lucas shakes his head. DeBusschere shakes his head.

Dean Meminger comes in. He mentioned something about playing in college, and fights breaking out.

"The college kids are all hepped up for the game," said Meminger. "They only play one or two games a week. The coach says, 'Don't you guys take nothin' from the other guys.' So they go out there like bulls and see red."

DeBusschere said, "A lot of times it's the referee's fault. Especially homers on the road. They call these terrible charging fouls." Then Dave, wearing only a jock strap, impersonated a referee calling a charging foul—slapping his right hand behind his neck, pointing with his left hand and skipping across the floor. It broke us up.

"In college once a guy called that on me," Dave said. "'Get your hand up. Get your hand up.' I said I didn't foul him. I'm not getting my hand up."

Phil Jackson comes in. "How come, Luke, they didn't give you any time last night?"

"Arrgh," said Luke. "After the show I did my tricks for 'em. Great, they said, great. The greatest stuff we've ever seen. Come back next week. I told 'em to forget it."

"Right," said Whelan. "The show around the corner's the answer."

Pretty soon, everybody's there. Although once in a while you get a crisis. For a home playoff once against Baltimore, Phil Jackson was missing. Everybody was supposed to be in the locker room at 7:00. The game was starting at 8:00. At 7:15 Phil Jackson had not shown up. Whelan called Jackson's home. Jackson answered the phone. He had overslept. Jackson came barreling into the locker room at about the same time Whelan was putting down the phone.

I tape my own ankles. Since college I've been taping my ankles. Most guys let the trainer do it but I took courses in athletic training at Southern Illinois. It's good to know, I think, because your

Taking the E train to work.

ROCKAWAY PARK
F
8TH AVE

A woman on the subway platform asks for an autograph. She found a pen, but she had trouble locating a sheet of paper.

body is your business. And to know how to take care of injuries could save you from missing a game. Like most guys, they turn an ankle, they never keep ice on it all night. They neglect it somewhat. The next morning the ankle is really swollen. Whereas I know if you get on it right away you can minimize the swelling.

Bradley likes the trainer to rub him down before a game. I rub myself down. I get the analgesic balm on my legs. It's soothing. I'll put the balm all over my arms, too. I wash my hands and put my uniform on.

It's 6:45 p.m. I wear two pairs of clean socks, socks that fit, that don't slide back in your shoes. Both pairs are pretty heavy. They give me a good cushion. And I wear heel cups in my sneakers. It's like a little cup you put on your heels to prevent you from getting hurt if you ever come down too hard. I once had a bruised heel. I haven't had one since I've been using the heel cups.

It's a matter of pride in the way you look. It's always been that way for me, like in football in high school I always liked to dress to look good. My coaches always liked to have us looking good. My high school coach said that the teams that look good usually play good. Even when I was in college, the coach was conscious of the colors and how the team looked on the floor.

So I make sure that my shirt is tucked in and my socks are right and my shoulder straps aren't twisted. Once the game starts you've got to forget about that. But I found that when my shirt was baggier I'd be fixing it at the free-throw line and it would bother me, throw my shot off.

Some guys, like Bradley and Phil Jackson, don't much care about appearance. Jackson's shirt always seems to fall out and Bradley's socks always droop. We kid them about it, but they don't seem to care. Whereas Barnett and myself are particular. I have all different color combinations of Puma Clydes. I have pairs for practice and pairs for games. I guess during the season I use about twenty pairs. Whenever I feel I'm not getting good traction or they feel loose, you know, I change. When I wore a different

On the way to the Garden locker room.

style sneaker I used to wear Knick-color strings. orange on one shoe and blue on the other. Something different from a conventional white. I don't usually wear strings like that on my Pumas. The sneakers are colorful already. But I see some kids with the different-color shoestrings on Pumas. They look good.

Sneakers are a special thing with people. Calvin Murphy, for instance, said he will never change from Converse. When he was a kid growing up in Norwalk, Conn., he could only afford those buck ninety-five specials, the ones that have the sole flapping out after you run down the court once. When he made his high school team his coach took him downtown to get some good basketball shoes. They were Cons. He was thrilled, but he says it almost ruined his game. He got so dainty he didn't want to move. He said he didn't want to bruise his Cons.

Some dudes wear black low-top sneakers for knottin' up. Go into some neighborhoods and even if you're wearing a suit and tie, you can't really strut unless you're wearing black low-top sneakers.

I used to wear high-tops when I played. I was afraid to wear low-tops because I twisted my ankle with them a few years ago. But recently I've played with low-tops and had no problem. I found it doesn't matter as long as your ankles are taped. And I think I can cut better with low-tops.

Now it's about seven and I'm all dressed. I go to the mirror. Most of the guys do that, go to the mirror before the game. I guess I spend the longest time there. Bradley will just go when someone reminds him to comb his hair. So he'll

Jerry Lucas and I arrive early in the locker room.

give a couple flicks and he figures he's ready.

Just before going onto the floor I like my hands to be dry, so what I do is rub them on the bottom of my shoe. I think all players go through a ritual before they play. A lot of guys say they aren't superstitious, but in a way you are because you go through the same routine. Like if I had a good game, I'll go back to the same restaurant to eat. Something like that.

When you're on a winning streak you always want to do the same thing. Never change. The same thing. I've had good games and my sneakers need to be changed because they're wearing down, slippery almost, but I won't change now. Not until I have a bad game. Like in the playoffs when we lost a game to Los Angeles, Danny Whelan our trainer made everybody sit in a different spot in the locker room. When we'd come in he'd say, "Get over there in the corner, Clyde." Everybody was spread out in a different place. That's superstitous.

I seldom sweat but maybe this game is making me a little more nervous than usual. It happens. Bill Russell used to vomit before big games. Maybe I'll have an extra couple drops of perspiration. So what I do is spray some pit juice on. My beard and mustache are good for soaking up perspiration. Some people think it's a handicap. It's not. On the court you get used to it and don't even know it's there.

Some people say, well, how can girls want to kiss you when you have a mustache and beard? It's like what Archie Moore the old fighter answered to that question. Girls are thrilled to go through the forest to get to the picnic.

But my mother convinced me to shave off my

beard. She said it made me look like I was not her son but her grandfather.

I'm not like a lot of players. I don't like things hanging on me. It distracts me. I have nothing extra on. Like Abdul-Jabbar wears a medallion. I think medallions are dangerous. Say you go in for a layup and that thing is flapping in the air and a guy grabs it.

Monroe wears two wristbands. Wilt wears a lot of stuff on him, a headband, a kneeband, a wrist-band, a rubberband on the other wrist. I figure if it doesn't bother a guy what is it as long as he can perform. But even if I have an injury I hate to have even tape on. Other than on my ankles. Throws my game off. I feel like I'm in a straitjacket.

Just before going on the court I'll do a few little exercises, like stretching and touching my toes and bending my knees. Cazzie Russell, when he was with the Knicks, went through a whole routine with isometrics, calisthenics, jumpingjacks, running in place, push-ups, sit-ups, knee-squats and some other things never before seen by the naked eye. Someone once asked Dick Barnett how he prepared for a game. He said, "I watch Cazzie for about five minutes and then I'm ready."

When we go on the court I warm up just to the point of feeling ready. I always start warm-up shots close to the hoop. Some short jump-shots, some layups, some longer jumpers. When I feel ready I dribble along the side. Then I sit down. I warm up just to the point of breaking a sweat.

Changing clothes before the game, with Earl Monroe and Dean Meminger. The film of the last game against this night's opponent is seen.

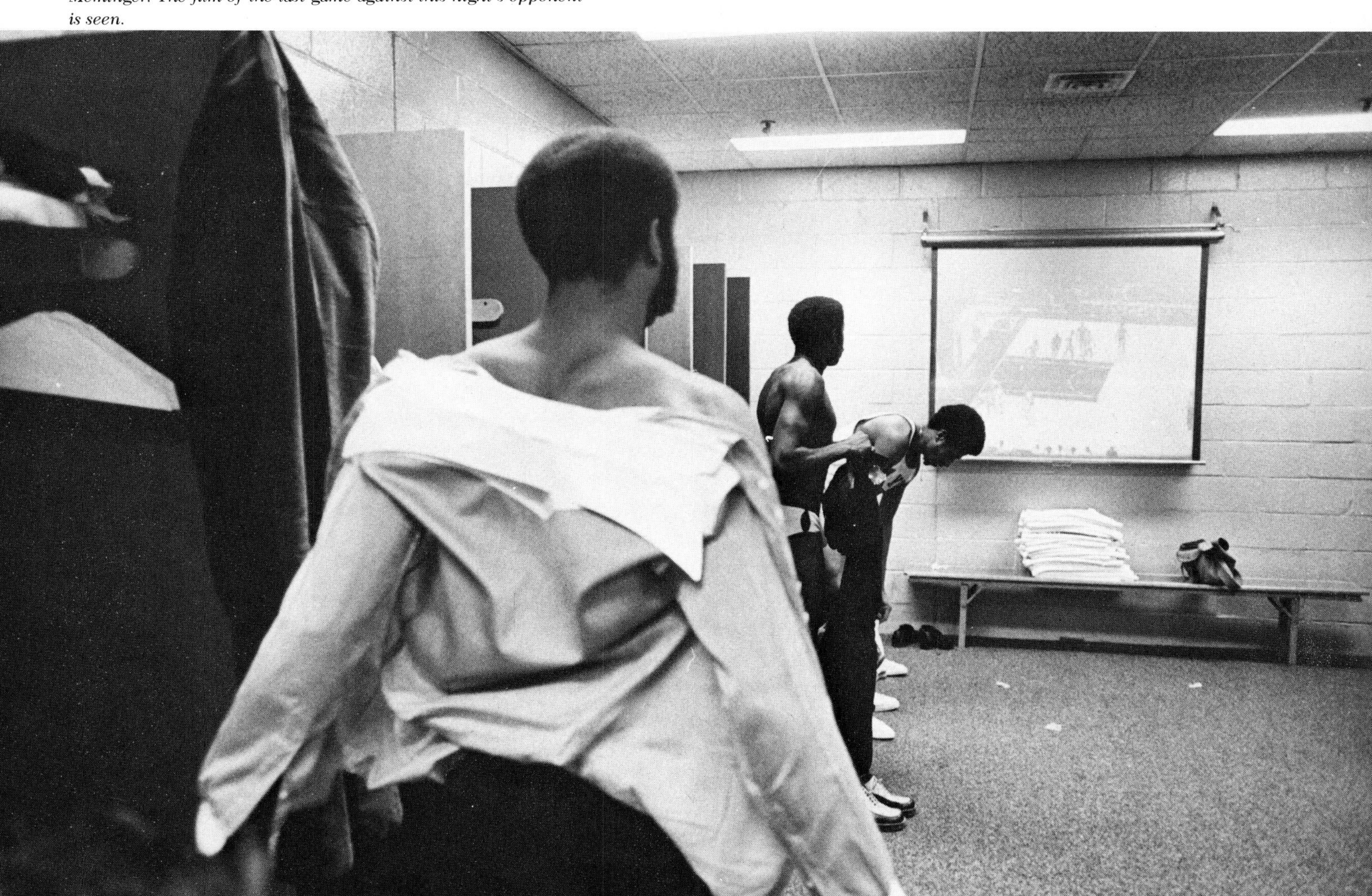

NEW YORK

Vitalis

I found that whenever I break a sweat and the game starts, I'm tired. It seems as if all the excitement is gone from me. If I'm too psyched up before the game, then everything is downhill from there. So I wait until the game starts and then I build up a peak.

Just before the game starts I like to cool off. I wet a towel in cold water and dab it on my face. It gives you a different feeling. Similar to taking a cold shower or something. I rub my temples and hold my neck back and creak it around.

I'll pop some gum in my mouth. A fresh half a piece for each half of the game. Keeps the mouth moist. I think it helps me not to be thirsty. I found that chewing a whole stick of gum made me hungry. That's why I now chew only a half a stick at a time.

The introductions are made and I hear my name. I like the sound of it—"Walt Fra-zier." And the crowd cheers and I'm getting lifted up in my sneakers and I'm getting readier for the game. I trot out.

But some games you can't get in to—the rhythm, like you can't really get the rhythm. I've had games where you get three fouls early. You sit down. Then you come back in, and it's not the same. I've always found it hard to come off the bench. The game's on 78 speed and you're on 33 1/3. You just can't get with it.

Some games I'm not psyched up until my man starts to score on me. Then I get a little bent out of shape—unhappy—and it jogs me. Or some games I get psyched up by making a good shot or a good move. Or a good steal or a good pass. The crowd roars and I'm flying.

Like all athletes, I've had games when I thought I choked. Games where I can tell when my shot's off or I didn't handle the pressure like I know I can. But you're going to have games like that: You have the key shot and miss it. You're at the free-throw line and you miss, and that could have won the game. That's a choke.

Or some games where normally when it's tight in the last minutes I'd like to have the ball, only I don't go for it now because I don't have the feeling I could make the play. I don't take the challenge. That's choking.

It's choking when you don't want the ball under pressure. You can tell the guys that don't want the ball in the last five minutes, because when the game first starts and you're the ballhandler you can see everybody's face. They want the seed. But when the game gets tight you see only their number. Everybody is going away from the ball. Nobody wants it.

When I'm taken out of a game I don't want to cool off too fast. So I put on a jacket or a towel over my shoulders and over my legs.

A lot of people wonder why I sit on the floor so long after I've been fouled and knocked down. Some people think I'm hurt. Some think I'm mad. What I'm doing is cooling off, relaxing my body. This is especially so under pressure, when you'd normally be tensed up. I'm getting my head together for the free throw. I know there's no hurry to get up. So I cool it. When I walk to the line I'm ready, mentally ready to drop the ball in the hoop.

I'm not one for tricks. Guys still use tricks. Like on defense if a guy goes up for a rebound some defensive players might hold his shirt or step on his foot. All those things eventually are going to provoke a big hassle. Or he's going to tell the referee to look out for that and once they find you doing it they're going to start making that particular call.

Some guys try to hold your shorts. I don't know of anyone who's had his shorts pulled off on the court yet but it might happen. The guys grab pretty tight. Most of the big men do that. They try to keep you from running down on a fast-break. Some guys who are out of shape just stand around and hold you.

Some players have reputations for being dirty but there aren't that many left today. Everybody's trying to make a living. But there are still certain ones you got to watch out for—like when I go in for a layup I'd better protect myself because I don't know what they might do. Some guys will try to hurt you; they'll try to go under you on a drive, low-bridge you. Well, I'm always under control. I anticipate them fouling me. When I jump for the layup I jump so that I'm still on balance. But if a guy goes under me I forget the basket. I'm going to make sure I'm coming down right. But you see a lot of guys still follow the ball. That's how Cazzie Russell broke his wrist. He jumped and his feet were still behind him so he landed on his wrist.

One guy you have to watch out for on layups is Happy Hairston of the Lakers. Guys know he'll bang into you when you're in the air. There was a big thing made of the fact that Kareem punched Hairston when they played in a game on national television. Kareem went in for a drive and Hairston banged him from the back. I saw it on TV, too. I saw Kareem look to see who hit him. If it had been a West, say, Kareem wouldn't have done anything, I don't think. Because Kareem would have known it was an accident on West's part. But Kareem saw it was Hairston and he duked him.

I'm always aware. If a guy goes under me I'll throw the ball at the stands or something. But most guys know that if you have a shot they shouldn't bang into you.

On rebounds, a lot of the taller guys, if they get me under the basket, will try to put an elbow on my shoulder so I can't jump. They're just lazy. Eventually they get called for that. I try to play the game the way it should be played, without illegal hips and elbows and sticking a finger in a guy's eye. It makes the game more fun. And you don't go out on fouls as much.

Free throw.

Under the hoop for two.

A lot of guys fake fouls. I hate that. Jerry Sloan's the worst. Like when you come down on the fast-break you pass the ball out and he's standing in front of you. You'll step away from him and then he'll fall. He's always falling. He gets blown over by wind drafts.

Guys on defense fake-fall a lot from picks, too. If it works I guess it's okay, but the danger is what if a foul isn't called. Then the man is gone for the basket.

On offense I don't fake fouls because I usually know when a guy is going to foul me. I fake him up when I have the ball and then I jump slightly ahead and our planes cross. Foul on him. Jimmy Walker has a trick on offense. He'll shoot the ball and then he'll come down on your shoulder and sometimes they'll call a foul on you. Some guys when they shoot and the ball goes short they scream to the ref that you hit their elbow, even when you haven't touched them. But some guys do try to hit the elbow. Pistol Pete said that the first advice his coach, Richie Guerin, gave him when he came into the league was that he'd have to learn to shoot with guys hitting his shooting elbow. I don't do that. I'm concentrating too hard on playing good defense. And when I'm shooting I never try that fake call. I'm so shocked when my ball doesn't go in that I'm speechless.

I don't talk much on the court, except to my own men. A lot of the talkers, the psychers, are gone. Like Sam Jones. If you made two or three baskets in a row he'd say, "Slow down, son, you're shooting too good tonight." They'd try to say little things to throw your mind off the game.

Dick Barnett still talks a little. Like when I first came up to the team Dick would make a shot and tell his man, "Too late." Or when he'd shoot he was famous for saying, "Fall back, baby." Like he knew the ball was good and so he's telling his teammates to get back on defense. "Fall back, baby."

The worst I think was Bill Sharman in the 1957 All-Star game when he threw a full-court pass to Bob Cousy that went in the basket by straight luck. Sharman turned to Dick Garmaker, the opposing player nearest him, and said, "You never could play defense." (Cousy came back and said, "Bill, you're a good shooter but a lousy passer.")

It could be embarrassing to a guy, telling him he's too late or something. But it could have an adverse effect in that it could really get a guy mad and he'll want to guard you that much closer. So I think that's why today guys don't say much. Like if you've got 30, 35 points on a guy you never say he's a poor defensive guy. You just say, "Well, I had a hot hand." What's done is buried.

I very seldom complain on the court. I've never had a technical foul called against me. I know when you're angry you can't play good. You're out of control. Like Bradley, when he's angry he just makes a lot of bad passes and crazy stuff. Willis gets very physical and gets into foul trouble. In the 1971 playoffs, I couldn't believe how Jack Marin let the crowd destroy his game. He had had a fist fight with Phil Jackson in Baltimore. Now the Garden crowd was on Marin in the next game. He went wild. Technicals. Wild shots. He just should have sat down and dabbed a cold wet towel on his temples. I remember Luke Jackson once when he was with Philadelphia and got this rebound and his elbows were flying and he was gruntin' and snortin' to scare people off, and he swung his arms around and the ball accidentally flew into the stands. He was embarrassed.

It's funny, but I'm usually better than ever in the last five minutes of the game. That's when the game is often won or lost. Even if I play a poor game up until then, sluggish, I usually do something that might win the game. I'll steal a pass or make a basket or pluck a rebound. Pressure usually psyches me up.

When the game is over I like to unwind. I usually have the reporters around me because I've done something spectacular in the game. I wear a towel around my shoulders so I don't cool off too fast. I go through a ritual after every game: A ballboy comes over and I'll have a cup of water and two or four salt pills, depending on how I feel. And I'll have some apple juice.

Post-game interview.

Some guys, before the game is over, are in the shower and gone. I don't think anything is that important that I have to rush. Especially when you had a good game. I wait for the mimeographed statistics sheets to come and be passed around. I sit down and read them—savor them. You think how well you did it and then you start thinking about the next game. But when we lose, a funny thing happens. The stat sheets are in the locker room in no time flat, like they were printed up before the game. I want to kick them away. When we win the stat sheets always seem to take an hour to get there.

My problem is that when we lose I always think I could have won the game if I had done something different. I think about maybe one move or one shot—like if I don't take the last shot in a 1-point or 2-point loss, I think I should have. I think about it all night. And even in the next day's practice. But also I might see the game films and say, "Oh wow, I didn't have a chance to do that," to do what I had been thinking in my mind I could have done.

In every game there are always some moves I liked, that stick out—I liked that shot or that steal, something like that. It might be offensive or defensive. So I replay those slowly in my mind and maybe someone like Lucas, who lockers next to me at the Garden and who is a late dresser, too, will say something. Like I remember after the

Post-game toast at Harry M's, with my business manager, Irwin Weiner, and friend, Toy Russell.

first game of the 1972 season Luke had 12 assists. That's supposed to be my job, assists. But I guess he was struttin'. He said to me, "Don't get open, Clyde, or I'll give the ball to you." I said, "I'll give it right back."

In that game the one move I enjoyed remembering most was a play when Luke and I came down on a two-on-one fast-break and he was in the middle and passed me the ball on the side and I gave him a perfect lead bounce pass back. He sank the layup. It was a beautiful play.

Now it's like. 10:15. Everybody's gone. I shower, dress, go through my mirror routine, get my gear together and leave. Often I'll drop into Harry M's, a nice bar and restaurant on street level in the Garden. Lot of the players and my business manager and friends go there.

Some nights I'll go home early. I'll hop a cab (traffic's no hassle now) and get back and take a hot bath. That's usually early in the season or on a night when my legs are achey, like after a third-or fourth-straight game.

Other nights I'll maybe meet a friend and tuck in early. And then some nights, if we don't have a game the next day, I'll go dancing, especially if we win. I like to celebrate. I still have a lot of energy. It's funny. Like I've played 48 minutes and I've gone and danced at discotheques afterward for three, four hours straight. You just sort of get with the beat of the music and you rock steady into the night.

REX
MAD

A general guide to looking good, and other matters

1. GROOMING SECRETS

a. Every morning that I wake up I go through a routine. I get out of bed, stand and bend low from the waist. This gets the blood to flowing through the body.

b. Then still in that position I give my head a finger-tip massage. Then I pull my hair, and knead my scalp. This is good for the circulation of the head and hair. Not long ago my hair started falling out. I got a book on how to save your hair. It was a necessity. Can you imagine a bald Clyde?

The book's suggestions have straightened out the problem. After the massage, I use the 100-stroke system with the brush. All this takes about five minutes, and it all takes place in the bending over position.

c. I take a lukewarm shower, then a cold shower. Stimulates the blood, and that's good for the complexion.

d. I dry my body with a stiff towel, and use short brisk movements. That beats the blood up, too. But I use a soft towel on my face, and I dab. I don't rub, that irritates the skin.

e. I don't use much soap on my face, maybe once a week at the most. Soap dries the skin out.

f. Every morning I squeeze a towel with water as hot as I can stand it on my face. Then I use a cold towel on my face. I rotate this about two or three times, a minute for the hot, a minute for the cold. It helps circulation by opening and closing the pores.

g. I don't usually like lotions on my body because it makes my clothes feel sweaty. But I sometimes use Noxzema on my face.

h. I slap cologne all over my body: lookin' good, smellin' fine.

i. I keep my fingernails short, for two reasons. One, I don't want to cut up somebody on the court. Another is that I wear a lot of knits, so short nails is an economy move. I'm afraid that with long nails I'd be tearing up my clothes.

j. I do facial exercises. I stretch my mouth—it looks like I'm yawning. I blow up my cheeks, like I'm carrying two cheekloads of water. Those two exercises help keep the facial skin tight.

I also squinch my eyes very tight, and then I open them wide. That relaxes the eyes.

I do the eye and facial exercises whenever I have a spare moment. I avoid doing it in places like a crowded elevator. You can get some pretty queer stares.

2. BREAD

I spent a lot of money when I got to the Knicks. I never had much money before. Now I had some. I signed for $25,000. I spent about $10,000 in clothes my rookie year. Funny thing is that I didn't really want to spend the money. But I didn't know what to do with it. I was out there, floating, searching. I needed some financial advice and I didn't know where to go for it. So I bought clothes. That pacified me.

Everybody has to have a hangup. Mine is clothes. Some guys have drinking or smoking or cattin' around. I've got clothes. By my second year my bank account was disappearing. I was getting worried. I was getting a paycheck and didn't know what to do with it. I had one financial adviser and he didn't do me much good.

Then I met Irwin Weiner. Irwin was the head of an organization called "All-Star Sports," in which top athletes from New York in all sports formed this group for endorsements and public appearances. Before, some of these agent quick-buck artists would take an athlete to make a public appearance. The athlete would get, say, $500, while the agent pocketed $1,500. The athletes were in charge at All-Star Sports. I became a member. Irwin would pick me up and drive me around to make appearances. I didn't say much to him for six months. Good morning. Thank you. Good night. But I was checking him out. He seemed honest. And I liked him. Soon I was letting him handle a few of my affairs. Then more and more. Now I trust him with everything. He's negotiated my contract with the Knicks, which is great. We've built up Walt Frazier Enterprises. Irwin has done great negotiating work for guys like Julius Erving and Bob Lanier and Johnny Neumann and Luther Rackley. He taught me about getting money "up front" on a contract, instead of in deferred payments like a lot of guys who may not collect all their money until they're sixty-five or something. And if their franchise goes bankrupt, they're out their money.

Anyway I've now got a million dollars in liquid assets—that means, in cold cash if I want it. So you can understand why my nickname for Irwin is "Wonder Weiner."

The main thing is that we're very conservative with investments. We stick with municipal bonds, that sort of thing. My slogan now is, "It's not what you make, it's what you keep."

3. MY OWN MAN

Whatever I believe is right, that's what I do. I don't care what everybody else is doing around me. There are times I went to parties in high school and guys would want me to drink. I didn't drink. They'd say, "Drink it or wear it." So they would pour booze on you. A lot of times that would happen to me. Like guys were drinking and

One of my three vine-yards

they'd get drunk and they would get jealous because I didn't drink. The times I tried to drink I didn't like it. I'd say, "I don't like the way it tastes." They'd say, "You aren't supposed to taste it." I'd say, "Then what am I drinking it for?"

When I got older I used to drink Scotch, Scotch and water. And I'd always have a terrible hangover. I think it was my rookie year that I gave that all up. One night I was so drunk I went to bed and felt like I was going to vomit. I crawled on my hands and knees to the toilet and leaned over the bowl. Nothing happened. I crawled back to bed. Felt like I was going to vomit again, crawled back to the toilet, leaned over again. Nothing. I was in tremendous pain. I felt it could happen at any time, so I decided to sleep right next to the toilet bowl, right on the washroom floor. Slept there all night. That's when I said to myself, "What do I need this for?"

I don't need grass, either, because I can sky on myself. But I like to drink wine. I drink wine because it doesn't affect me. I can drink it all night and the next morning I can go to practice and run and I don't feel like throwing up. I don't wake up like some guy is beating me on the head with a hammer.

I'll smoke a little cigar when I'm frontin' it. A Tiparillo or a Hav-a-Tampa. They smell sweet. I don't inhale. I just puff. It's a cool to go with a Clyde outfit.

In college I used to smoke a pipe. I found it very relaxing. I never smoked a pipe in public, it wasn't my image. Too stuffy. But in my room I had a problem studying. I was a physical-education major (I still have thirty credits to go before I get my degree—I gave up my senior year to join the Knicks) and I'd be studying and my mind was over in the rec room, what's happening there. I'd be thinking I might be missing something. So I could never really completely concentrate on my studying. I would fumble with a pencil or something.

I had a roommate who smoked a pipe, so I tried smoking a pipe. I'd smoke and puff and my concentration was right there. My grades improved a lot. Once I smoked a pipe, my mind never wandered. Maybe it was all psychological, but it helped me. I became a connoisseur of pipes and pipe tobacco. I'd always buy the most expensive tobacco because I didn't want a bitter taste on my tongue. I had about eight different kinds of pipes. When I wanted a short smoke, I had the small ones. When I was studying I wanted to puff maybe an hour or so, I had a big one. But I gave them up when I became Clyde.

4. FOOD

No way you can be cool and be fat. So I hope to stay in shape all my life, stay slim and trim. Because I know that's the secret of life. Like they say, some people eat themselves to death. I'm interested in health foods. I used to sit there and eat a lot of potatoes and bread and feel like a stuffed sock. I'd feel worse after the meal than before. So now I very seldom eat a lot of starchy foods.

I used to love sweets, still do. Like apple pie and ice cream. I've really cut down. Now I can go into a restaurant when the guy brings the sweet tray around and I can pass it up with my stomach, even if I can't pass it up with my eyes. So I'll eat fruit for dessert.

I also bought a calorie-count booklet to carry around. When I have a question about what to eat, I refer to the booklet.

I don't normally eat breakfast during the off-season. And sometimes I may not eat lunch. I found I often get dizzy if I eat breakfast. But if I happen to wake up early I might have breakfast. It's usually Granola or some other pre-sweetened health cereal. Sometimes I'll just have an apple. I drink health-food milk, which is unpasteurized and comes in a black carton because sunlight can't get in and sap the vitamins out of the milk. I take a lot of honey. Sometimes I'll have it on an English muffin. Sometimes I'll drink it straight out of a jar. And some mornings when I think I'm coming down with a cold I'll take a cup of warm water and put a tablespoon of honey in it. Every morning I take a thousand milligrams of vitamin

C and 100 units of vitamin E.

For lunch, once in a while in the off-season, I'll have a milkshake. For dinner I try to stay with fish, liver, turkey, steaks, eggs, cheese and chicken—food that's easy to digest. I eat about four to five hours before a game. A typical meal: cup of chicken soup, tossed salad with French dressing, steak medium, glass of ginger ale, couple of french fries, fruit. If I eat too early I'll be hungry in the last quarter of the game. If I eat too close to game time, then I'll feel sluggish, and then I'll play bad for maybe three quarters. Like I'm walking in my sleep. People move by you like you're standing still. Then I wake up in the fourth quarter. And I'll hope it's not too late to save the game.

Some guys drink water or soda at halftime. I've even seen some guys eat at halftime. When I was a rookie, there were guys who didn't care about the team or themselves. They'd get the ballboy to bring them a hot dog.

I try to stay off water during and after a workout. I drink water in the mornings. Then it doesn't bloat you. Sodas don't quench your thirst. I used to drink four or five sodas after a game. Now I bring my own organic apple juice and I put it in a cooler for after the game.

When the game is over I'll eat something light, like a sandwich, so it doesn't lay like a rock in my stomach when I go to sleep.

5. WEIGHTS

In college I started lifting weights a lot. I was nearly driven to the weight room because I thought I was very weak and a lot of guys were

I still lift weights, even in my living room.

jumping over my back for rebounds. That used to get me mad and I figured the only way to stop it was to get stronger.

The year I was ineligible for varsity basketball in college I'd be working in the weight room and then I'd come out to play a choose-up game of basketball. I'd realize how strong I was getting and I'd rush right back into the weight room. Guys started calling me "Superman."

My coach, Jack Hartman, was afraid I'd get musclebound. But I didn't lift so much that I became bulky. I worked out about four hours a day. I did isometric exercises. I did curls and bench presses and toe raises. I did a lot of squats to strengthen my thighs and calves. I got advice on what I should do—what my body was capable of with exercises and weights—from one of the phys-ed teachers.

In college off-seasons, I'd try to get the most difficult physical jobs. One summer I was a construction worker, carrying cement, lumber all that stuff. Another job was in a cotton factory. I was truckin' 500-pound bales of cotton. I wore ankle weights the whole time.

I also did a lot of running. I don't think any of this made me jump any higher. But I think it helped me jump quicker. Instead of jumping one time, maybe I could jump two times for a rebound.

Once the season started and Coach Hartman saw how it really helped me, he put all the guys on a weight program. Not four hours a day like I did, just a couple hours a day. But you see, if you're going to work with weights you have to really get into it. Their minds weren't ready for it. They didn't feel they really needed it. So they didn't work at it. Most basketball guys don't think they need it. I thought I did. That makes a difference.

I still follow weight and running programs in the summer. I still run two miles a day and do windsprints during the off-season. Every morning I loosen up with eight windsprints up and down a football field. The first 50 yards I build up and the last 50 yards I run all out.

I always try to get my form together, you know, being smooth. I'm running under control, but running pretty fast. Like a game. Keep pushing, keep driving. Like you do eight laps, the last two are tough. So I say, last five minutes of the game, gotta make it.

Some mornings I don't feel like working out. But I know I have to do it. Same with weights. I can curl 65 pounds. I can only bench-press about 100 pounds. In the summer I do three sets of curls ten times, with rests in between, fifty squats, some other stretching exercises.

It doesn't have to be drudgery, working out. It can be fun. I enjoy working with weights almost as much as I like playing basketball. You have to envision your body getting stronger. And you have to like what you see in the mirror. I see the definition. Lookin' better than ever, Clyde. That's worth the work.

6. THE RACK

When I was younger I thought I had to sleep twelve-thirteen hours a day to get my basketball rest. Now I only sleep eight. Someone like Lennie Wilkens says he only sleeps four hours. I found out when I was younger that if I'm active during the day, doing things, moving, I'm usually more relaxed and alert and I play a lot better when the game starts. Except on the road.

On the road I'm catching up on my rest. First thing I do when I get to a town is buy a paper and get the TV guide out so I can budget my TV time. I look to see what good movie will be on and then I just fall back in the rack.

I sack out all day. It drives my roommates batty. Like John Gianelli.

When he was a rookie he wanted to see all the new cities. But I don't get up 'til late. So he got up early for breakfast and I'm still in bed. He comes back. I'm in bed. He goes out for lunch and comes back. I'm still racked out. He goes out to see the sights, afraid to miss anything. But I've seen them. Well, I get up about two-thirty, go downstairs, have some lunch, come up and climb

The Clyde super-bed

Clyde

back into bed. John returns and he sees me *still* in bed. All my roommates, they never say anything but they get this funny look on their faces every time they walk in the room and I'm still tucked under the covers. Sometimes they'll come in and stand real quiet, to listen if I'm still breathing.

One morning in Seattle I couldn't sleep. I was up and walking around at about 8:30 a.m. Well, John wakes up. He opens one eye and sees me. He does a double-take. "*Clyde,*" he says, worried, "what time *is* it?"

On the road you sometimes run into bad beds. There are the humpbacked and the slopes and the rocky roads. So when you're home you make sure you're comfortable. So my bedroom has to be special. I've got a nine-foot round bed with a fitted white mink bedspread. I have a matching nine-foot round mirror on the ceiling. My back wall is one big mirror and in the right-hand corner is "Clyde" in script sandblasted on.

I have a wall-to-wall shag carpet. White silk wallpaper and white silk drapes cover the window. Behind those drapes is a purple-painted wall and a purple window shade. I have a chrome dresser, two night tables: one glass with chrome legs and the other redwood. I have a chrome lamp, a color TV. There is a complete stereo unit in my den and speakers are wired throughout the pad. The stereo has FM-AM radio, with eight-track cassette tape deck, turntable, tape recorder. I have a pair of earphones next to my bed. It's not hard to relax in that room. And if I ever get bored just resting and meditating and listening to sounds, I can always gaze up at myself in the mirror. The only problem is I have this crazy fear that one day the mirror will fall down on me. Well, you have to take the bad with the good.

7. IN PRACTICE

They say, "You do in practice what you do in a game." That's true for high school and college. You work on plays and fundamentals in practice and try to use them in games. I took practices very seriously. It's a time to work things out. But not so much in the pros. You play so many games that practice is usually just to get loose. Say I play 45 minutes on a Tuesday, and so will Bradley and DeBusschere and Reed and Earl. Then we'll play a game on Thursday. But on Wednesday we have practice. Red wants to work on something. So the regulars play the subs. They're fresh, and they mop us up bad.

8. YOUNG CLYDE

I never got professional advice. The only thing that I got was just playing ball in the schoolyard at the Forrest Road Elementary School. One thing that helped me was we played on dirt, not asphalt. So that saved a lot on my legs. I also developed my dribbling there. You had to be a pretty good dribbler just to handle the ball, keep it under control because of the rocks and bumps on the dirt court.

I was fortunate that I always played with older guys. You learn by playing with good competition. I started basketball at about nine years old. When I was eleven I was playing with guys who were twelve and fourteen. And I was good for my age, so the older guys took me under their wing. I was always a little taller for my age, so I didn't worry about growing—like, say, a Pistol Pete Maravich did. And I never thought about hanging from a door to try to grow like he did. (I don't think it really works, anyway.)

I can remember shooting for nickels. I didn't have money but I can remember the other guys did and I would shoot for them. It was pressure but to me it wasn't too much because it wasn't my money. We drew a line about fifteen feet away from the basket. You shoot from behind the line. You make it, the other guy misses, you win a nickel. It made you concentrate.

Maybe you can say my basketball career began in the eighth grade when I was working at a curbside restaurant. When someone drove up, I got their order. But a few of us set up a kind of basket in the back. We nailed a big malt cup to the wall. Then we crumbled up a smaller cup and tried to throw that in the "basket." We never got fired for this, but there were some customers who wore out their horns.

I was a very naive kid coming up. So I try to make my brother, Keith, who is ten years younger than me, aware about certain things in life. To do things that turn out best for him the way things turned out best for me. I was very shy and I think I missed a lot. He's quiet, too. He's in to athletics, baseball and basketball, like I was. But I tell him to talk to people. You learn that way. I only opened up from my shyness my last two years of college. I started to talk to professors, for example. It was a trip. I'll try to enlighten Keith, but I'll never force him. Like my son. I'd never try to make him a basketball player. He's a good athlete already. I can see he's coordinated. But he'll be what he wants to be.

When I go back to Atlanta now, I get a perspective on things when I was just coming up. I lived in a segregated city but I don't think I missed much except education-wise. When I went to college, the freshman courses were refresher courses for most of the white kids—they had that stuff in high school. But it was all new to me. So I was behind and I suffered for it. I was shy and that hurt, too. Like in my speech class. I shook when I had to give a speech. But I said to myself, how can you be afraid to talk in front of twenty people you know and then go out and play basketball before thousands of people you don't know? So that cured me and I started to enjoy giving speeches in the class.

I go back to Atlanta now and I see the hotels that the blacks weren't allowed in. Those hotels used to be hot stuff. Now they're nothing. All run down. And Georgia Tech gymnasium was a real white groove when I was a kid. I played there the last few years against the Hawks and I hated it. It was the dingiest place in the NBA.

I never had a run-in with white people when I was young. I've never been one to go where trouble was. I was a homebody, like I've said. I've

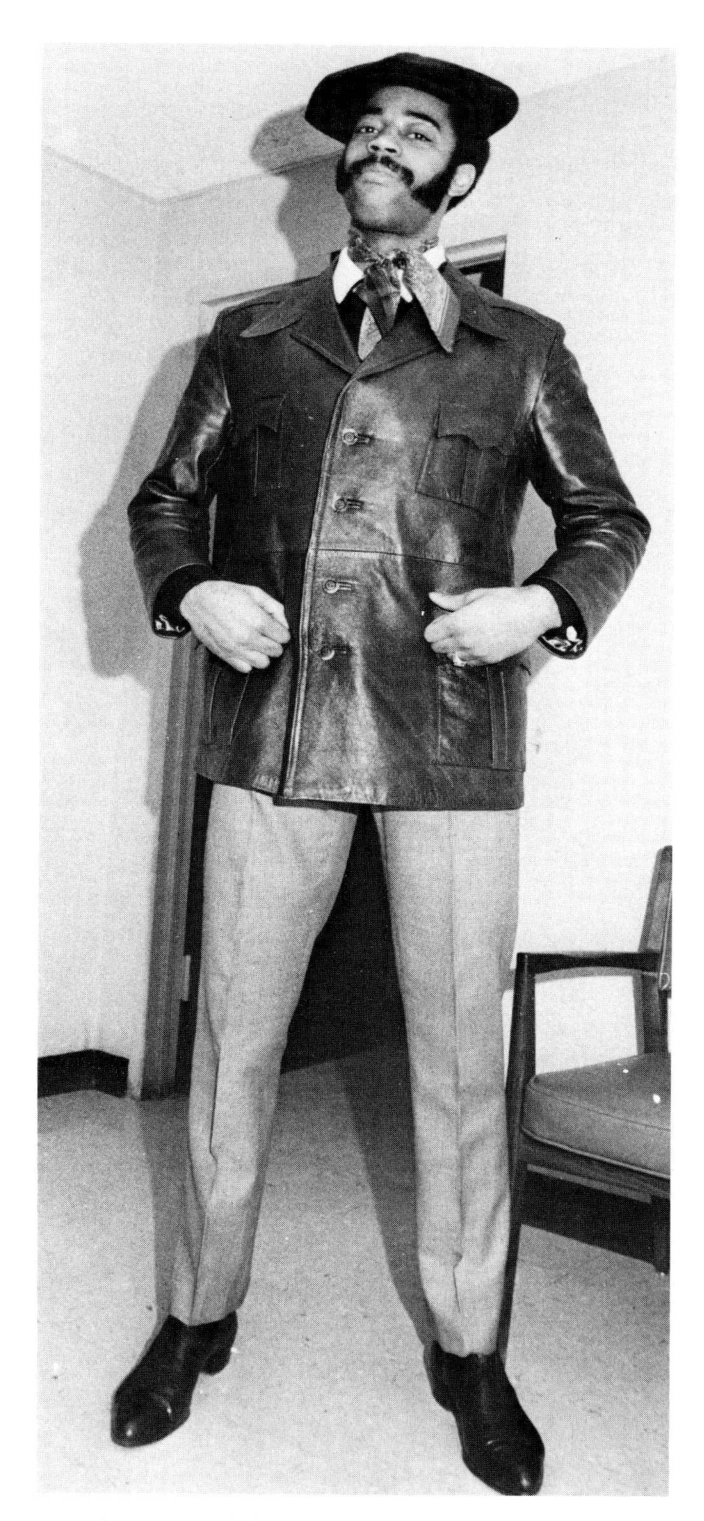

An earlier, pointier Clyde look, circa 1970

never been locked up and very seldom in trouble. Like I might be called nigger but I was never in too many places where they could call me nigger for long. If somebody was calling me nigger they would be riding up and down the street in my neighborhood, maybe coming from a ballgame. But I would always mind my own business. There were places or neighborhoods you knew you shouldn't go, but other guys would. They'd join gangs and things like that. I was a loner, like I am now. Maybe I had one good friend then, like in high school, one good friend in college and one or two good friends that I bounce around with in New York. Usually they aren't athletes. They're just guys I met and liked and trusted. And I go off with them.

Funny thing, but it was being black that determined my basketball career. When I graduated from David T. Howard High School, I had more football scholarships than basketball offers. Indiana wanted me, along with some other Big Ten teams. But even then I was thinking of the pros someday. I knew there were no black quarterbacks in the NFL. That decided it.

That situation is changing in the NFL. But I think I was lucky. If I had it to do again today, I'd pick basketball because there's a lot more money in it.

But I think I liked football more. Running the team intrigued me. You'd run a dive play to set up a sweep. Then you'd throw in a fake and pass. Basketball is so fast, you do something and it's gone. So I have to rely on my memory so I can savor some of the beautiful moments on the court later.

9. LOOKING AHEAD

I know that all this fame and glory is not for ever. One day I'll fade from the scene, I'll go back to just being plain Walt Frazier. There will come a day when people won't be coming over to my table in a restaurant and saying. "Clyde, thank you for the pleasure you've given me when I watch you play basketball."

I found out in college what you can expect from most people. I didn't make grades and I started being treated like dirt. If I asked the coach for a ride somewhere, he'd say get one yourself. If you can't do anything for some people, then they don't want to do anything for you. In college, that just inspired me, made me mad. When I was in high school, something happened that gave me a perspective on all this, on what you can expect from people when you're an athlete and don't produce.

I was the second-string quarterback in the tenth grade, until the No. 1 guy got hurt. That was at the beginning of the season. Well, I didn't know how to handle the team. I was too young and inexperienced. I came in the second game. We lost that game and all the other games that season. We didn't win before me and we didn't with me that season. People called me a bum. I didn't ever want to show my face at school in the mornings. In my senior year I was the quarterback. I was throwing perfect 50, 60-yard passes. I threw 16 TDs. We won the city championship. Things changed. It was cool now. I was a hero. And I enjoyed that. I was voted Most Popular and Most Athletic in my graduating class. But, still, I never forgot the tenth grade.

10. HEROES

I never had a real model when I was a kid. I was always my own type player. There were no guys on the playground that I wanted to be like. Most kids have idols. I was different. I never saw a pro game until I was in college. Whereas these kids today have watched a hundred pro games on the tube already, and they're like nine years old.

I only had idols from what I read in the papers. Like Mickey Mantle or somebody in baseball. When I played baseball I saw different guys in the Southern Association that I tried to copy, like the catcher who caught with one hand in his pocket. In football I liked Johnny Unitas. I thought he was cool. Did his job great and didn't fat-mouth about it.

Pogo

I started watching some pro basketball games on TV when I was in college. They came on at one or two o'clock and we had practice at four, and I'd try to incorporate moves I saw into my game. I always watched Hal Greer for his good moves. And I tried to do some similar things, like dribbling left-handed down the left side of the court, then crossover dribble, go around the pick and then jump-shoot from the top of the free-throw circle. On defense there was Jerry Ward of Chicago. He was the best. He'd be in the game and he was all over his man, getting over picks. So that was impressive to me.

Some people compare me to Oscar Robertson. I never idolized Oscar and I never wanted to be like him, but I wanted to be good. I admired Oscar's passing and consistent jump-shot but I never tried to shoot like him because it wasn't my shot.

11. ON BEING AN EXAMPLE

The only thing about me that I'd want kids to identify with is that I'm my own man. I don't use people and I don't let people use me. I've got my personal style, and that's me.

I don't preach to kids that if they keep their nose clean they will grow up to be Clyde Frazier and be cool. What's important is that I don't make a big show.

Some people have called the successful black athlete a "cruel deception" because then black kids try to be athletes and forget about school. And a lot of kids, they say, who fail in the sports dream, end up on the street, or worse. Well, to make any kind of success in athletics, you almost have to go to college. Basketball and football have their farm systems, practically, in college. And baseball is going in that direction, too. So black kids who want to be athletes have to go to college. Before, not many black kids—athletes or otherwise—went to college, could afford college or were allowed in. But going to college, that's what is important if the black man is to get ahead.

I believe what Bill Russell says: Kids can look up to a black athlete as an athlete, as someone who has worked hard and developed his talents, a man who has accomplished something he wanted. But a father should set an example for a kid, or an uncle or a religious or neighborhood leader. My example is that I'm Walt Frazier. I do my job well. There's only one of me, just as there is only one of you. I always try to remember who I was, and who I am. Once certain people get to a certain position, they change entirely. I've known guys I worked with in college and all of a sudden one would be made a supervisor of the dining room and he can't even talk to you anymore. We used to break bread together, and all of a sudden he's changed because he has a title. I don't dig that.

I've been in places and people say, "What are *you* doing in here?" Like I'm supposed to be above that. The public puts you on a pedestal and they can't see you doing normal things. They think you're supposed to be someplace else. Even somebody else. That's one reason it's hard to have good friends, men or women. Too many people look on you as an object, a thing you like wind up. All they want is to introduce you to their friends: "Like you to meet Walt Frazier, the basketball player." What should I do then, spin a basketball for them? I used to hang out in Harlem a lot and people would say, "That's not Walt Frazier!" They figured I was supposed to be on the East Side, swinging.

You have to be careful where you go. I go out a lot, frequent a lot of different places. But there was one nice place in Harlem and I'd go there, then Ned Irish, who owns the Knicks, called me and said, "Walt, I hear you're hanging out with undesirables." I said, "Who?" so he told me so-and-so and so-and-so. Well, they'd wanted to shake my hand and buy me a drink. So maybe we'd talk about things in general. So maybe you're a crook. I don't know that. That's how Joe Namath and Bob Cousy got in trouble. So now I try to stay out of certain places because it's bad

for the image. I've met people who say all kinds of things about you. One time I was supposed to be pushing pot. Always rumors about you. And the places that swing are the places with the pimps and the hustlers. This is where the action is and you're considered guilty if you're just there.

But I have a lot of reasons why I do a lot of things. I deal with blacks and I deal with whites. People always sell that "brother" stuff. Like in business deals. I've got burned a lot by my own kind—as well as the other kind. So now I go wherever is best for me. That's self-preservation.

Trying to drive against Jabbar.

12. ONE-ON-ONE GAMES

I think they are great for developing moves but not to the extent where you're just a one-on-one player and can't play with four other guys. I play one-on-one, it gives me a good workout during the off-season. I can work on my jump-shot. When I play I don't stand in one spot. I keep moving around to different angles on the basket. Sometimes I shoot the ball at the rim, sometimes I bank the ball, sometimes I set a guy up for a drive. I'm doing a lot of different things. Even if I have to lose the game, I don't like to just stick with one thing, one favorite shot.

Like I might be able to beat some smaller guy by just backing him in, but I know that in actuality I'm not going to do that in a game. So very seldom do I try to drive that much. I'm a guard, I have to shoot outside. So that's what I work on, that and my defense.

Even if I play a guy bigger than me and he just keeps backing me, I just let him shoot. You know in a real game it won't happen. I can get help and steal the ball. Like when I played Julius Erving. He needed a basket and put his back to me. I just stepped back. What could I do? I let him have the basket. If you take one-on-one into a team game, it can hurt. I've seen guys see another man open but they'll shoot anyway with two guys hanging on. That's just being shot-happy. That's all in the way you're brought up. It carries over into the pros.

Competition, the pressure, psyches me up. Like in one-on-one I can still have a good time playing a guy who's not as good as me. Maybe I'll make the score 9–5 in his favor. And we play eleven baskets wins. Then I'll try to come back, tighten my defense, get my offense together. That's fun. But when you start playing for money, it becomes a different thing. You get a lot of fouls. The guys argue because they don't want to lose. You can be more competitive but it might not be fun. Like in college, I used to play a guy for breakfast. Whoever lost would buy breakfast. It didn't mean much to me. But I know guys who lose and they'll start pulling your hair.

Coach Red Holzman

13. GOALS

I know some guys make goals before the season to spur them on. I don't. I'd like to average 20 points a game, 8 assists a game, that sort of thing. But if you think too hard on that you might put unnecessary pressure on yourself. The goal gets too heavy.

14. THE COACH

I think he has to treat everybody the same, no pets. That's one reason I respect Red Holzman. I think he plays his best five men, no matter who they are. If he takes them out of a game and they fuss and pout, he'll tell them to leave. If they don't do right in practice, he'll tell them to leave. There are no prima donnas. Like Red is always on me. Especially on defense. He's always hollering, "Get back, Clyde." Once he hollered this and I wasn't in the game. I was sitting next to him on the bench. I said, "Red, I'm right here." He said, "Well, so you'll know for the next time."

Red Auerbach of the Boston Celtics likes to do a pregame psyche-out job. He's the general manager now, but he's got his coach, Tom Heinsohn, doing this one particular thing. You see, the visiting team has the choice of baskets to start the game. Red likes to have the Celtics come out onto the floor after the home team. The home team is already warming up on one basket. He figures that that's their favorite basket, the one they want to give them a good start in the game. Every team has a favorite basket, usually out of superstition.

Red or Tom comes out and blows off steam that he wants to start on the basket that the home team is already shooting on. So now the home team has to take its balls and go to the other hoop. He figures he'll distract your team, making you move, getting the upper hand right away. We know this. So what we do is warm up on the basket we don't want anyway. We do this all the time with them.

15. KNOW THE RULES

Once I used to say, "That's the coach's job." I felt my job was just to play. But my mind changed when I almost lost a game early in 1973. A new rule in the NBA says you can't call a time-out in the last two minutes of play while moving the ball up in the backcourt.

I didn't know this. I was double-teamed. I called time-out. The other team got the ball. It was a close game and we're lucky that my bad play didn't cost us the game.

The same kind of thing happened to the Celtics in the fourth game of the 1972-73 playoffs. They were two points down with less than a minute to go and called time-out. We got the ball, held the lead, and won the game.

16. DON'T LOOK BACK

Like in high school, whenever you hit a good team and your players are all standing around and watching the other guys dunk the ball before the game, you get psyched out of yourself. I've seen teams watching us. That's a sign of fear. Like when we won 18 straight in 1969. You saw guys staring at us before the game. Instead of warming up they're standing around watching you instead of concentrating on what they have to do.

17. CATCHING A FLY WHEN THE FLY IS IN A SITTING POSITION

It's technique, not just amazing hand-quickness like most people think. Most people grab straight for the fly. That's wrong. You have to sort of curl your hand backward and slowly circle the fly. Then you come around in front of him. You have to be careful and patient, then move your hand forward and he'll fly right into your palm.

18. CATCHING A FLY WHEN HE'S IN MIDAIR

Amazing hand-quickness. But I seldom perform these feats anymore. Like I said, my reputation's out. Flies won't come within ten feet of me anymore.

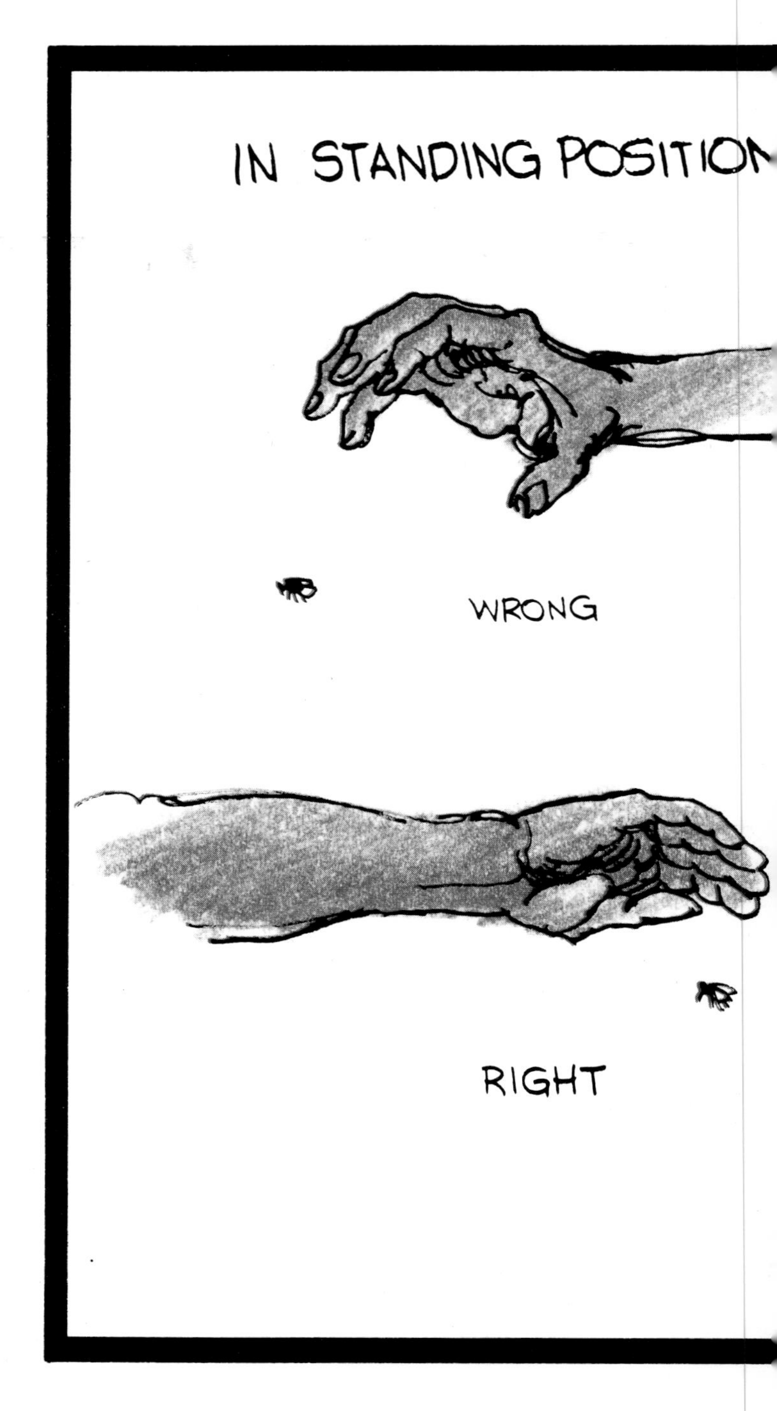

IN MIDAIR

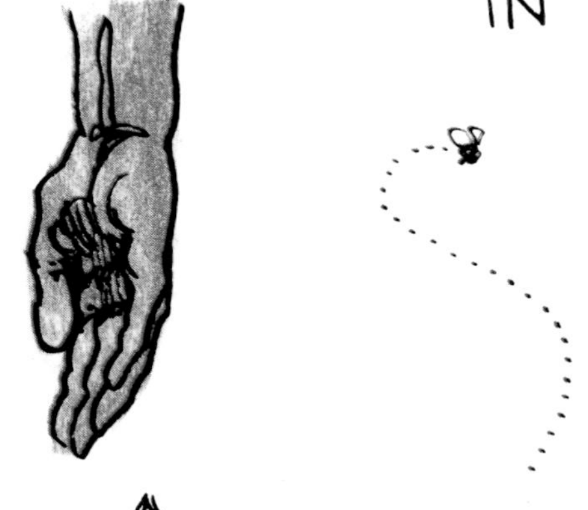

A

RELAX — CONCENTRATE
ON TARGET.

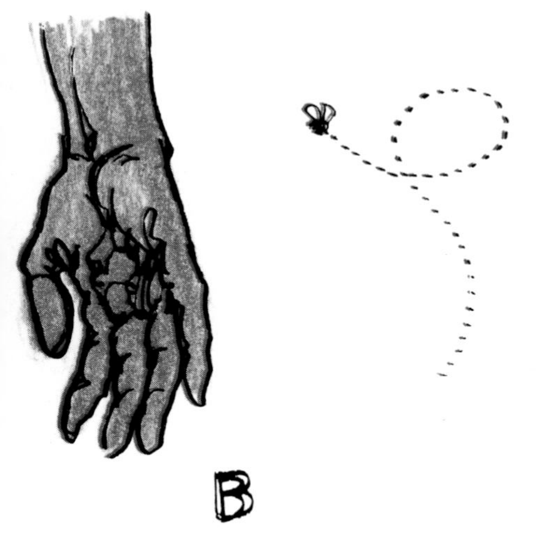

B

NEXT, BRING FLEXOR
ND EXTENSOR MUSCLES TO
SPRING-LIKE TENSION.

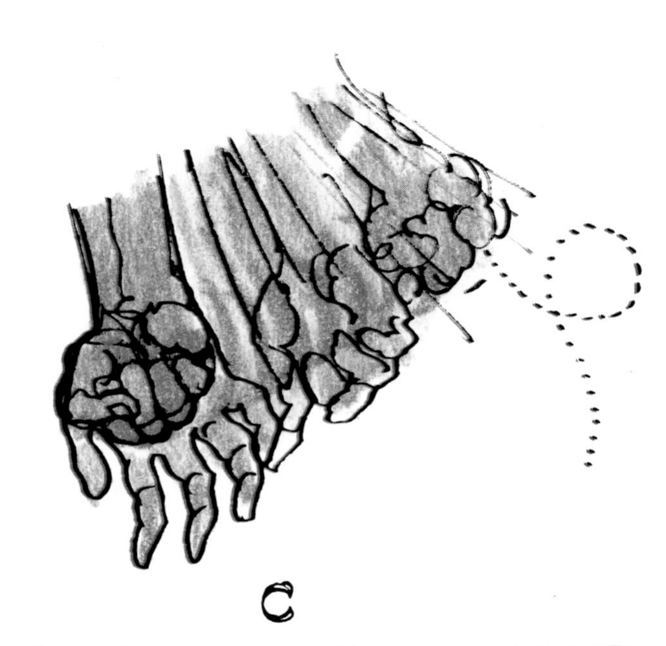

C

IF THESE MUSCLES ARE FLEXED
HARD ENOUGH THEY WILL AUTOMATICALLY
RELEASE JUST BEFORE TENDON
SEPARATES FROM BONE.
SINCE COMPLETE CONCENTRATION
HAS BEEN ON THE FLY, HIS
CAPTURE IS A MATTER OF COURSE.

19. OTHER SPORTS

I've mostly given up playing other sports. I hate to lose, and in other sports I don't usually have the concentration. I'll play pool with a friend and he'll beat me 4 games to 2. I get mad. Or I'll play Ping-Pong and I'll be leading and then my concentration goes and I blow the game. There's no such thing as "just for fun." I'm too much of a competitor for that. So now I'll be a guest at a house and someone will want to play pool or Ping-Pong. I'll say, sorry, I'm retired.

20. WOMAN

They go by what they hear, so I'm sure I get a lot of women just on my name. They hear I'm cool. They read magazines. But I also meet girls that don't know I'm a basketball player. They might see your dress, they think you're cool. So those are usually the women I end up liking because they are liking me for me, and not for basketball.

When I meet a chick I dig, it's like on the basketball court. I might not show my true emotion. I just might stare at her, saying nothing. It's like when I make a foul and really get mad, I try to keep a straight face. But inside I'll be saying, "Damn, Clyde, stupid fool." And I might stand with my hand on my hip and really look cool—while I'm getting myself together. Or when I hit a big shot I'll say to myself, "Cool move, Clyde." But I still got on my mask.

So now I'm just checking her out. I see how she reacts. You can usually tell if a girl likes you. If she starts turning shy you've got a pretty good chance to talk to her. Some girls I like because they have nice moves. I like the way they dance. Or I'll like the way they talk, some of the things they say. A lot of girls I meet say they couldn't care less that I'm a basketball player. Most wish I wasn't, so that they could have more time to spend with me. I'm sure that meeting Walt Frazier is a big thrill, but if these girls didn't dig my conversation, I wouldn't get anywhere, either. Whereas there are some other girls who think, "He's Walt Frazier. He can get any girl." So they try to be hard to get.

Looks are important but not the main thing. To me it's conversation. If we can communicate. When I meet a girl, very seldom am I serious. I like to clown around. Some girls are very sensitive and can't take that, so I know that's the person not for me. There are a lot of things I'll say but it's just a joke and they'll take it personally. I'll call a girl up and say, "Do you want to go out tonight?" She'll say, "Yeah." I'll ask, "When will you be ready?" She'll say, "In an hour." I'll say, "Do you think you can get beautiful in an hour?"

If I hear a click I know that she can't.

I often invite a girl to my game. I'll say, "Do you want to come and catch my act?" If she doesn't know me, she'll say, "What act?" If she does know me, she'll say, "Which act?"

You can't let anyone take your concentration off the game, and you can't let anyone sidetrack you. I should have learned my lesson in high school. I remember when I walked this girl home. We had a big game that night, a championship game. But I walked her home, three or four miles. We blew the game. I knew I could have played better if I'd gotten my rest. I cried after we lost. I cried because I knew I could have played better.

Now, the day before a game I never see girls. I stay home, maybe I'll cook for myself. I do anything but do it alone all day. I maybe take the phone off the hook. I completely relax. During the playoffs I don't go anywhere for two months. I figure a month, month-and-a-half, what is it, I can do that.

When I was younger it didn't matter whether we had a game, I'd stay out late the night before and party. But since I've gotten certain recognition, I want to stay being the best. So I don't take those chances anymore. I always want to be mentally and physically ready. And that's another reason I won't hassle over tickets anymore. My business manager handles that for me. Before a game some guys will promise six girls tickets and they have only three tickets and they're chasing around the locker room trying to find three more. You can't relax that way. By the time you scrounge up your tickets you've wasted all this energy and motion and you're ready to take a shower and go home.

My problem is that I'm not a hound. I don't chase girls. I go to a party and survey the premises. If I don't see any women I like, I won't say anything. I might just sit there and fade into the music. Or I like to watch people dance. Maybe I have a few drinks and then I'll split. A lot of poeple think that's being stuckup, not mingling. I don't want to talk basketball. A lot of guys come over and they want to rap about basketball. At a party, that's a bore.

Funny thing, a lot of guys' wives come over and say, "You made me a basketball fan since I saw you play." Or a guy will say, "My wife loves you. She saw you play and now she's hooked." That's cool. I'll say "Thank you." You know then people are really enjoying what you're doing. And in a way we are entertainers. It's nice to know you're appreciated.

I don't go out that much on the road. There is a certain type of girl that I like. If I don't find her, I go back to my room alone. It's very seldom that I'll take anything. But in some cases I might end up with something I don't want. But like I've said, everybody gets caught in a weak moment.

I'm not a long-distance man. I've met girls on the coast but I know I won't be back for another year, so why communicate all the time? I just throw the numbers away and start fresh next season. There are very few cities that I have steady girls in.

Most guys usually keep a girl in every city. That's not like me while I'm working. My main thing is playing a good game. My main objective is getting ready to play a good game.

21. ROMANCING

I pick my spots. I figure the way you start is the way you end up. So if you start out like romancing once a week, and now do it twice a week, it's going to affect you. I found that to be true. So what I do is, if I start out one way, I maintain it the whole season. My body is conditioned to that, starting from the summer though the season.

I think in basketball you have to be in better condition than football or baseball. Like Joe Namath said he slept with a blonde and a bottle of Scotch before a big playoff game. In football you can do that. The quarterback, for example, is not usually running anywhere. He's just dropping back, right? He doesn't have to run up and down the field the whole game.

It's like baseball players. Take Mickey Lolich. He's a 20-game winner and look at his stomach. It touches the ground when he pitches. But a baseball pitcher, all you have to do is keep your arm in shape. Those guys drink a ton of beer. It doesn't bother them. But if they tried to run up and down a basketball court, you'd have to carry them out of there in a wheelbarrow.

21. VINES

It doesn't always work out that if a guy is cool on the court he's going to be cool, dress cool, off the court. It happens to be that way in my case. But most guys are not into vines as much. Like my casual dress would be dapper for a lot of dudes.

Take Bill Bradley. We laugh at Bradley because he doesn't care. On trips, guys steal the shoestrings out of his shoes. He's walking around the airport with no shoestrings. He's laughing. Or he gets on the plane and we're walking up the steps and you see he has a big ice potato in his sock. That's what we called a hole in the sock when I was a kid. Or Bradley has a shirt on, there's a hole in the elbow. I figure he just does that to make people laugh.

Dapper Bill Bradley

He had this one raincoat where if it stopped raining he'd ball up the coat under his arm. It was bad. The first time we saw this was soon after he signed his bonus for half a million dollars. Red said why don't the guys chip in and buy Bill a raincoat. It was funny. Here are two rookies, him and me. One emptying out the clothing stores as fast as he can get to them, and the other guy, he could afford it but he's dressed like Harpo Marx.

There was one time in memory that Bradley came to a game dressed to the teeth. Everyone was shocked. We looked at each other. Some Princeton alumni were going to honor Bill at a dinner. So he wore his only suit. It's black. He also wore a pretty nice black coat with a velvet collar. I'll never forget those shoes. They were these big truckers and they were brown. They didn't match the suit. I don't even think they matched each other.

I was always conscious of being neat. My mother still laughs about how I used to spend half-an-hour ironing a pair of pants to get the crease perfect. And when I was going to wear a shirt or something that had been in the closet for a while, I'd press that before I wore it. And when the blue-suede-shoe fad came out I bought myself a pair. I was proud of them and brushed them all the time. My mother said I'd better be careful because I was brushing all the suede off.

My father was a good dresser and I would always try his shoes and shirts on. I was about twelve and the Stacy Adams shoes and the Nunn-Bush loafers were the style. My father had a lot of sharp clothes. He worked for the Ford Company as a factory worker. My brother has a thing about lookin' good, too. I send him a lot of my clothes when I get tired of them. Even my little boy, the Third, as my mother calls him, he'll see me and say, "Gee, Dad, I like that scarf," or something. He's really into clothes already.

In college I wore Ivy League button-down shirts, pants with skinny legs, penny loafers—the whole bit. I think my taste was always there but I didn't have the money for my type of clothes

Earl the Pearl

when I was in college. Then I signed with the Knicks. The first thing I bought were alligator shoes and some good leather shoes. I'm a shoe freak. Every week I'll buy a new pair of shoes. My closets are running over with shoes. I buy shoes and I have nothing to wear them with. I figure sooner or later I'll find something to match up.

Now I don't own any alligator shoes, or lizard shoes. Today the trend has changed. Ecology is part of it. Also, now the look is more square-toed, which is great for guys like me with big feet. I wear size 13, but I can wear size 12 in some European shoes. It varies on the make or the cut of the shoe. The only shoes that are really groovy now are high heels. At least 2 to 2 1/2 inches high. They're uncomfortable until you get used to them. At first it feels like you're going to fall over. Lately I've been having the heels cut down about a quarter-of-an-inch because I've been feeling a strain in my legs from walking.

I have about fifty pairs of shoes, from $35 to $100 a pair. When I'm overhauling my shoe wardrobe I give a lot of my shoes to a good friend in Atlanta. Otherwise I wouldn't have any room to walk around in my apartment.

My whole thing is, I don't try to keep up with the styles totally. That's how you go broke. Styles might change every year. So then your suit is out of style. I basically buy what I like. I like tapered suits because I'm tall and have a slim body. I think that's a good look for me. I have the wide lapels, which is the "Clyde" look. There, too, I go to different styles. I think my colors are toned down somewhat. I used to like loud colors, like light blue and reds. Before I went just for color, now I want my suits to have a good cut and a nice material. Like I told Max Evans, the fashion editor from *Esquire* magazine when I was voted "the best dressed jock," my taste is becoming very conservative. And I was wearing this one black outfit with a poncho and silver studs. Max sort of blinked and didn't say anything. (But he wrote that "It is not for nothing that he is known as Clyde, a name bespeaking dash....")

I think basketball players are in a good position because they have the bodies to wear certain type stuff that looks good. Whereas football players are usually too bulky. There are some football players that look good in their stuff. Those are the halfbacks or the flankers. I hear that Leroy Kelly of the Cleveland Browns is a pretty good man with the rags. I also know that Frenchy Fuqua thinks he's pretty hip to clothes. Frenchy wrote a letter to *Esquire* that dripped with envy after the Best Dressed list came out. The letter was entitled "Sour Drapes":

I used to think *Esquire* was cool, but your selections of The Ten Best-Dressed Jocks, August (1972), make me wonder if your fashion editor wears white socks and a key chain. Bob Gibson in that blue single-breasted jacket looked just right for attending a funeral. Rod Gilbert has looked better in his hockey equipment than in those threads *Esquire* thought dreamy. Take another look at that picture of John Mackey. You'll notice the photographer took pity on him and tried to hide his shoes. Our schedule tells me I have to carry the ball against Carl Eller this year, so I am not going to say anything about that Goodwill dashiki he wore.

I do not know which is more embarrassing—to have been omitted, as I was, from your selections or to have been included among that motley crew.†
Ask Pittsburgh about Count Frenchy Fuqua. Inquire about my lavender cape, my glass walking stick, my Three Musketeers hat with ostrich plumes. Watch for bulletins on the caveman look I'll be sporting this fall. Among those in the know, the Frenchman leads the way in any fashion parade.

(signed) Count Frenchy Fuqua
Running back, Steelers

†*The rest of "that motley crew" are race-car driver Peter Revson, skier Billy Kidd, Leroy Kelly of the Cleveland Browns, golfer Doug Sanders, tennis star Stan Smith and Gail Goodrich of the L. A. Lakers.*

Frenchy Fuqua

Clyde's Wardrobe Stats

Suits

(Based on latest change: Complete turnover every two-three years.)
Total: 49
(Excluding those in rear of my three closets waiting for exportation to family, friends, Harlem boys' organizations.)
Closet highlights:
1 goatskin, tan.
1 deerskin, brown.
1 green cowskin (with light green "x"-pattern stitching on collar, sleeve-ends, pockets and jacket hem.)
1 black cowskin, with poncho and silver studs.
1 white twill
3 lambskins: black, tan and baby blue.
Pockets in pants, none.

(Once I didn't have pockets for use anywhere on my suit. It was a trip getting used to. I bounced around with my money in a Puma bag and carried it over my shoulder. When I was really steppin' out, I'd give the money to the girl I was with; but that's risky. That's why I have inside pockets made in my jackets now.)

Pants

I usually wear pants from my suits even if I'm not wearing the jacket when I'm cas al.

A couple of closet highlights: 1 antelope; 1 deerskin.

Also, kickarounds, about 10 pair: jeans and corduroys.

Highlight:
Maroon cords with UFO patch on backside.

Sport Jackets

All suit jackets can be used as sport jackets.

Shirts

Approximate total: 50.

(Always in transition, hard to pick exact number because they are coming—on order or at a moment's notice when I walk out of the house—or going to friends, etc.)

Dress shirts, to order, about 35.

Closet highlights: solid chocolate brown French voile with white pearl buttons. Five buttons on each sleeve.

Black Swiss voile with gray yoke, cuffs, buttons.

Pink English cotton with white sleeves, collar, cuffs, pocket flaps.

Knots

Don't have any now. Ties aren't in style. And turtlenecks are acceptable almost everywhere. But when guys are going dapper for the night they'll still say they're knottin' up.

Kicks

Number, approximately 50.
Almost all leather or suede.
Colors, groovy.
Heels are usually between 2 inches and 2 1/2 inches.
Square or rounded toe, all.
Loafers, maybe 30: lace-ups, about 20.
Closet highlights:

Pink with a blue (matches my baby blue lambskin suit): a beige and cream: a dark brown and a green: a brown with a white.

1 pair brown cowboy boots (worn once—I'm keeping them until I hire two men to help me take them off whenever I wear them).

1 pair brown python-skin with gray suede around edges.

Belts

1 dark brown leather with wide brass buckle with "Clyde" in script on it.
1 black leather.
1 tan leather.
2 orgy belts, one white with brown and black figures; one black with white and brown figures.

Coats

Number, 7
1 black elephant skin.
2 sealskin: 1 natural tan Lakoda; 1 brown.
1 black full-length ranch mink, with eight double-breasted mink buttons.
1 dark gray cashmere.
1 British officer raincoat, with flared bottoms, epaulets, belt, flap pockets.
1 old raggedy trench coat for when it rains.

Lids

Number, 18

Most are "Clydes" (four-inch brim, about an inch or more wider than normal).

1 black calfskin gaucho.
1 brown calfskin "Riverboat gambler"
1 brown Clyde velour
1 green Clyde velour

2 straw Panamas (with wide band in several colors—I usually prefer red.)

5 summer Big Apple or Applejack caps (in old newsboy style), silk or denim: 2 yellow, 2 red, 1 blue.

6 winter Big Apple caps, cashmere or wool: black, burgundy, blue, brown, red, tan.

1 rumply white tennis hat.

Jewelry

I haven't bought jewelry in years. Have a few pieces, that's all. I wear a diamond ring and a Knicks championship ring, and a bracelet that says "Clyde" in diamonds.

I have a twenty-dollar gold piece on a gold chain, above the gold piece is a little white pearl with a blue evil eye painted on it. The eye is there to ward off evil spirits. It was a gift from a friend. It's like my good-luck charm. I wear it every day.

The "Count" wasn't critical of my vines, so his taste can't be as bad as he makes out. I mean, ostrich plumes?

In basketball, I think the guards dress best, then come the forwards. Last are centers. Your mental outlook is important in dressing—and like guards are usually cool around the court. But a lot of it is build. Now, Bill Bradley has a funny body if you really look at him. He's not in to clothes at all, but he'd probably look passable in Ivy League clothes. I don't say you should dress like me, but you can dress in nice taste in different-type clothes.

In baseball you see some guys with suits fitting nice. They are mostly outfielders. Whereas pitchers don't care. Their suits are baggy, they hang all out.

The thing a couple years ago used to be to dress up sharp, suit and tie. But today all athletes are casual. I don't know if I own a tie anymore. It's a whole different trend now. Everything is mostly mod today. I think I'm casual with just a shirt and pants. Now I have, say, a brown shirt with beige cuffs and beige collars, back yoke and beige "Clyde" across the sleeve. Most of my things say "Clyde" or "W.F." Ecology has influenced my clothes. But if a species isn't in danger of becoming extinct, I don't see harm in wearing it.

On the road I don't take many clothes. It's a hassle to lug all that stuff. Your arms are killing you. I carry my tape deck. Sometimes I have a clothes bag on a long West Coast trip. I'll have a suitcase with my uniform and my sneakers (usually blue with white stripe and orange with blue stripe) and my cosmetics. I always make sure I have my Colgate toothpaste—used it since childhood—and my Aramis after-shave lotion. I'll only take one pair of shoes. That's because I don't go out much on the road.

I don't like to carry my better clothes on the road. They get all wrinkled and crushed. Or like in Seattle it rains a lot. I'll take one color motif, maybe brown, something that I can match up with different pants. When I take brown pants, plaid pants or checkered pants then I can alternate the pants and coat. So instead of having one outfit, I have two or three.

One of the coolest athletes is Dick Barnett. He's a style-setter. Like some of the shirts you see today are two-toned. He wore them two years ago. High heels, they're the trend now. He had them two years ago, too. He's six-four but he would always put in an extra lift to have his shoes higher.

And he's cool on the court. He doesn't come across cool to kids or the public. I've never understood why. Even his playing hasn't made him the popular guy he should have been. When he first came to New York he was averaging 23 points a game. But the fans never really took to him. Yet here's a guy who is now past thirty-six years old and he's still a good player. He's smart, on the court and off. He's been going to school in the off-seasons and he got a master's degree in urban affairs. He's now going for his doctor's degree. He's very funny, too. He's got these stories about guys from his childhood that keep us rolling. Like the cool dude in his old neighborhood with one short leg. The cops were once chasing him down a street and they were catching up, so he got on the side of the curb to even himself out and got away . . . And Dick's got taste, and I go to his custom-shirt place, Altchiller-Friedman in Brooklyn. In fact, he's got so much taste that he now goes to *my* tailor.

Having things made is a beautiful thing. Right now I get a completely new wardrobe every two or three years. I have this deal with a clothing manufacturer, George Elliott Company. I get eighty pieces of clothes a year—that is usually forty suits. All I have to do for it is, when someone says, "Gee, that's a groovy suit, where'd you get it?" I tell them. And I take a few advertising pictures for the newspapers. It's a great deal but I wouldn't take the clothes if you offered me crappy stuff. I would have passed the eighty pieces up. I wouldn't wear a cheap grade of clothes even if they were free.

That's all the clothing deals I have, except for

my sneakers, the Puma Clydes. I test them out, make sure they're just right. They're a lot of money. You pay about twenty dollars for a pair. So I was telling them that the kids want a pair that's durable, that's worth the money. I think they are. At first I didn't think there was enough cushion in the sole. They improved that. They're a good sneaker. (Which reminds me that I once lost a sneaker in the last minute of a close game against Houston in 1973. I think someone stepped on it from behind and loosened it. But I didn't stop and scramble to tug it back on. I was guarding Mike Newlin. This is how Mike described it in an interview after the game: "I went to my right and I saw Clyde slip. Then I saw this shoe. It was just lying there. It had to be his shoe. It was orange. I'd been looking at them most of the game. Actually, I was usually looking at the bottoms as I chased after him." Mike figured that he could drive on a one-shoe Clyde. But I stayed with him even if it was like running on ice for me. He drove, took a double-pump and made the basket. It was a good shot. Johnny Egan, the Houston coach, said Mike would have made the shot even if I was wearing four shoes.)

I got a deal with the Seamless Basketball Company. They've got a Clyde Frazier ball. It's an outdoor ball that I use myself. It'll last. I don't endorse anything that I don't believe in.

Usually my deals are for one year at a time, because I figure that I get better every year and my name gets bigger. So rather than being tied up for three years, next year I come in again and maybe I get a better deal. You know, you have to take chances. Maybe they'll drop you. But you have to feel that you're in a position that you know you are going to get better every year. It's like gambling on defense. You have to have confidence in yourself.

I think I've also been lucky in business. You have to follow your instincts. It's like self-preservation. I don't blow my money, but I spend a lot, especially on vines. But I've made sound investments, things that will hold up the rest of my life. So I'm set. And that's cool. That's lookin' good.

There's one last style note that should be in. That is, always remember to wear your shorts on the basketball court. I say this because of something that happened when I was a sophomore in high school. It was the first game of the season. I was just on the launching-pad stage of being cool, so I was kind of excited. I had a lot to learn. Our team warmed up in sweatsuits. When I was ready to go into the game I began to slip off my sweatpants. I realized that all I had on underneath was a jockstrap. I had forgotten to put my shorts on! I had to rush to the locker room. People sitting in the first couple of rows from our bench were still laughing when I got back. So I learned this early: A big rule for cool is to get it all together.

Picture Credits

Walter Iooss Jr. All full color and black and white photography except as follows:

United Press International: pages 22, 23, 32, 34, 39, 42, 43, 44, 47, 48, 52, 55, 58, 71, 79, 81, 84, 99, 141, 146, 147.

Pages 12, 15, 16, 80 from Walt Frazier's personal album

Page 155; Courtesy of The Pittsburgh Steelers